PIONEER HANDBOOK

FOR ROYAL RANGERS
AGES 9, 10, 11

Prepared and edited by
Royal Rangers,
Men's Ministries Department
Assemblies of God

GOSPEL PUBLISHING HOUSE
Springfield, Missouri

02-0682

ACKNOWLEDGMENTS

Special thanks to the following:

- Ronnie Hembree, for writing the chapters entitled "Pioneering in Christian Service" and "Pioneering in Your Church."

- The Brotherhood Commission of The Southern Baptist Convention, for permission to use certain art work and to adapt certain stories and ideas from their Royal Ambassadors Manuals.

- Zella Lindsey, for the stories in the chapter entitled "Pioneering in God's Word."

- American Red Cross, for ideas received from the *Red Cross First-Aid Handbook*.

- Ralph Harris, for his help and suggestions in evaluating this handbook.

- Boy Scouts of America, for training and experiences I have received from my association with them—some of which is reflected in the terminology of this book.

Revised 1991

© Copyright, 1962, by
Gospel Publishing House

[PRINTED IN U.S.A.]

TABLE OF CONTENTS

Welcome	5
Let's Start Up the Trail	
How to Become a Recruit	6
The Royal Ranger Emblem	7
The Royal Ranger Code	8
The Pledge and Motto	9
Badges and Awards	10
The Uniform	11
The Pioneer Trail	
Second Class Requirements	14
First Class Requirements	15
Advanced Rating Requirements	17
Master Rating Requirements	19
Pioneering in the Out-of-Doors	23
Pioneering in First Aid	26
Pioneering in Physical Fitness	37
Pioneering in Your Outpost	43
The Patrol System	55
Pioneering in God's Word	67
Pioneering in Your Church	93
Pioneering in Christian Service	97
Pioneering in Your Home	101
Pioneering in Life	105

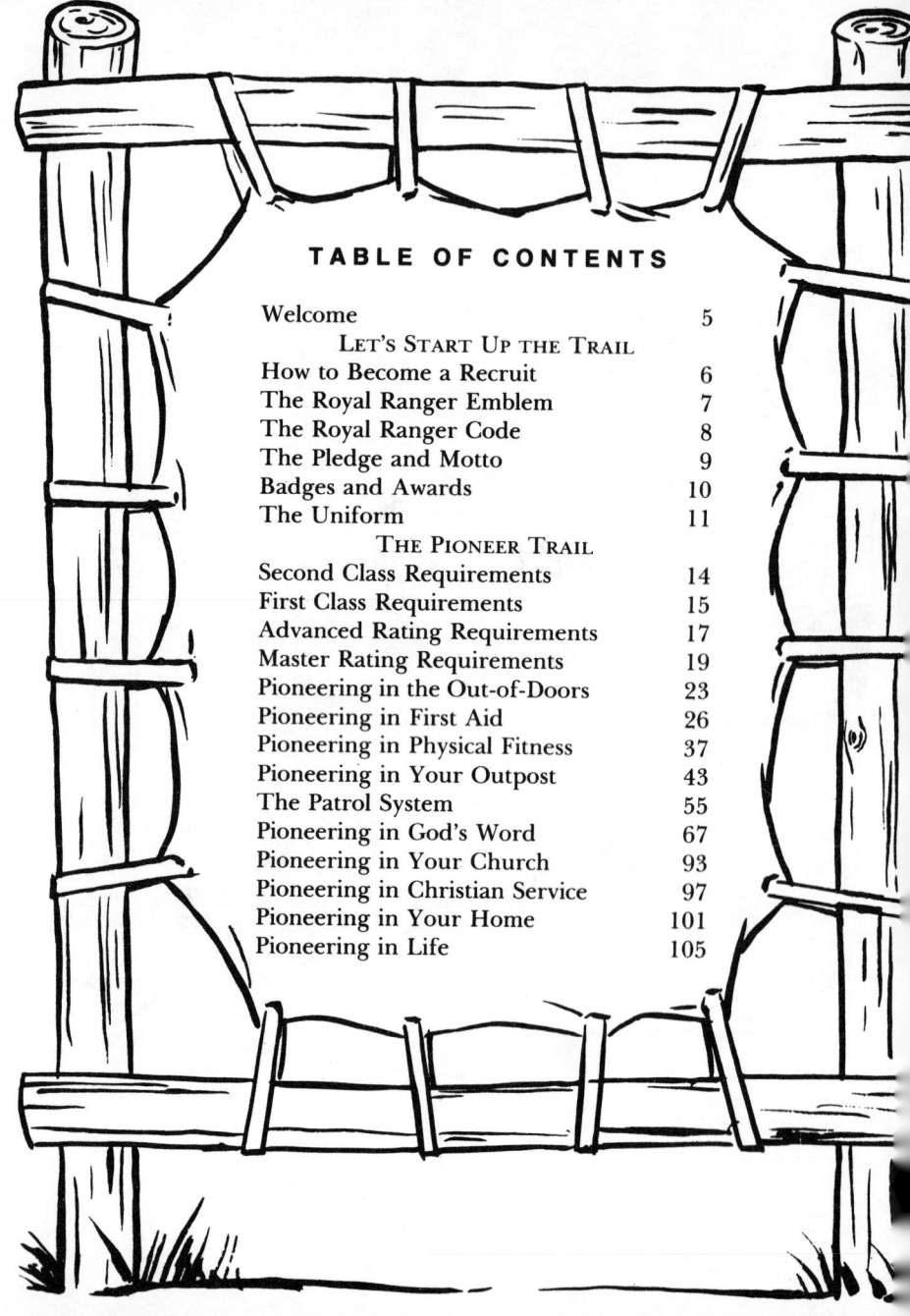

TO THE ROYAL RANGER PIONEER PROGRAM

You will have a thrilling experience as you travel along the Pioneer Trail. You know what a pioneer is, don't you? A pioneer is one who goes into new lands and places to blaze trails for others to follow.

The PIONEER HANDBOOK has been prepared to help you take part in many new and exciting adventures. It outlines the Pioneer program for Royal Rangers 9, 10, and 11 years of age. It will take you along the trail to activities in camping, hiking, first aid, games, nature study, crafts, physical fitness, Bible study, and service for Christ.

There are lots of exciting things ahead to do, so let's hit the trail.

LET'S START UP THE TRAIL

HOW TO BECOME A PIONEER RECRUIT

I. Be at least nine years of age.
II. Attend at least three outpost meetings.
III. Do the following:
    A. Learn the meaning of the points of the Emblem.
    B. Learn the points of the Code.
    C. Explain the meaning of the Motto.
    D. Give the pledge and explain its meaning.
IV. Attend Sunday school regularly. If you are not already attending Sunday school, enroll in a Sunday school.

ROYAL RANGER EMBLEM

MEANING OF EMBLEM

Four Gold Points—Four ways a boy grows:
Physical, Spiritual, Mental, Social

Four Red Points—Four Main Teachings of the Church:
Salvation, Holy Spirit, Healing, Rapture

Eight Blue Points—Eight points of the Ranger Code:
Alert, Clean, Honest, Courageous, Loyal, Courteous, Obedient, Spiritual

ROYAL RANGER CODE

A ROYAL RANGER IS:

ALERT
He is mentally, physically, and spiritually alert.

CLEAN
He is clean in body, mind, and speech.

HONEST
He does not lie, cheat, or steal.

COURAGEOUS
He is brave in spite of danger, criticism, or threats.

LOYAL
He is faithful to his church, family, outpost, and friends.

COURTEOUS
He is polite, kind, and thoughtful.

OBEDIENT
He obeys his parents, leaders, and those in authority.

SPIRITUAL
He prays, reads the Bible, and witnesses.

ROYAL RANGER PLEDGE

WITH GOD'S HELP, I WILL DO MY BEST TO: SERVE GOD, MY CHURCH, AND MY FELLOWMAN. TO LIVE BY THE RANGER CODE. TO MAKE THE GOLDEN RULE MY DAILY RULE.

ROYAL RANGER MOTTO

"READY"

Meaning of Motto: Ready for anything. Ready to: work, play, serve, obey, worship, live, etc.

THE GOLDEN RULE

"WHATSOEVER YE WOULD THAT MEN SHOULD DO TO YOU, DO YE EVEN SO TO THEM." Matt. 7:12

BADGES & AWARDS

MASTER RATING

ASST. GUIDE

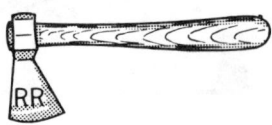

ADVANCED RATING

GUIDE

FIRST CLASS RATING

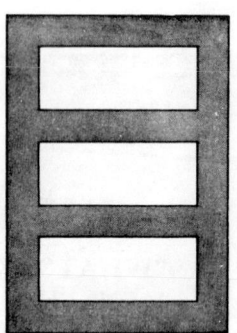

SECOND CLASS RATING

SENIOR GUIDE

YOUR UNIFORM

When you have completed the requirements for a Recruit, you are entitled to wear the Royal Ranger Pioneer Uniform (see illustration). It includes the Royal Ranger cap, neck-tie, belt, and insignia, worn with a khaki shirt and khaki trousers.

The khaki shirt, trousers, cap, tie, belt, badges, and emblem may be purchased from the Gospel Publishing House, 1445 Boonville Ave., Springfield, Missouri. Royal Ranger T-shirts, sweat shirts, and jackets are also available. Your Commander will have an order blank for all your supplies.

WEARING THE UNIFORM

After you have obtained your uniform, wear it correctly. There is only one correct way to wear the uniform and badges. This way is shown in the illustrations in the following pages. Wear your uniform with pride. Take good care of it. Keep it neatly pressed and clean. Hang it up carefully when not in use. See that your shoes are neatly shined when you wear your uniform.

Remember your uniform identifies you with thousands of other Royal Rangers in many places, so wear it with honor.

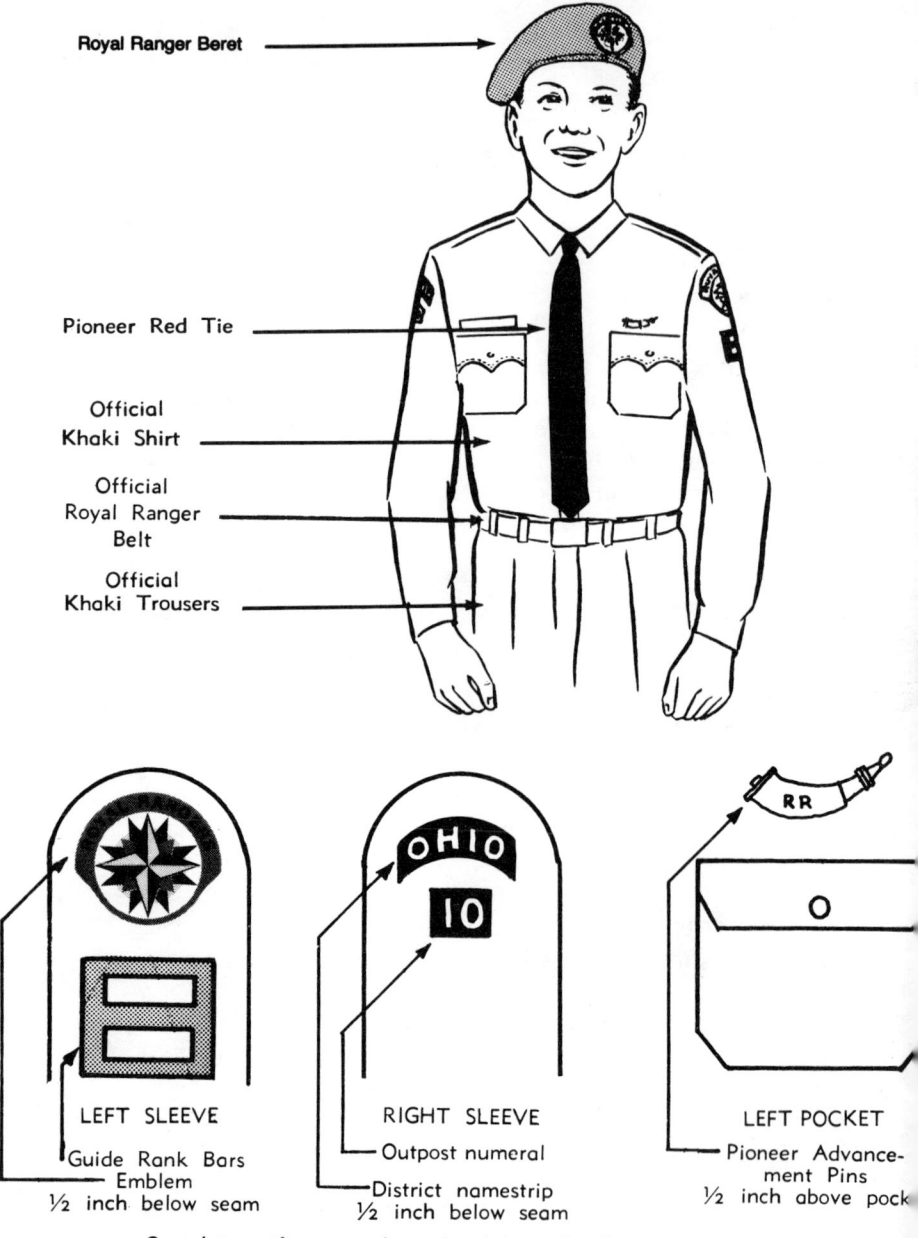

SECOND CLASS REQUIREMENTS

  I. Recite the code and explain the meaning of each point.
 II. Campcraft
    Under the supervision of your Commander
    A. Demonstrate how an area should be cleared before building a campfire.
    B. Build a campfire.
    C. Demonstrate how to put out a campfire.
    D. Explain why matches should not be played with.
III. First Aid
    A. Explain why cuts and scratches should be cared for.
    B. Demonstrate first aid for a minor cut.
    C. Tell how in an emergency you would get in contact with a doctor or hospital.
 IV. The Bible
    A. Explain how a person becomes a Christian.
    B. Read John 3:1-21 and explain what you have read.
    C. Memorize John 3:15-17.
    D. List three things a person should do after becoming a Christian.
  V. Service
    Send a card to six different shut-ins or sick people.
 VI. Your Church
    A. Attend Sunday school regularly for three months.
VII. Be a Recruit for at least three months.

FIRST CLASS REQUIREMENTS

I. Campcraft
   A. Cook at least one item over a campfire (building the campfire correctly).
   B. Demonstrate how to tie two ropes together so they will not slip, and demonstrate three other knots.
   C. Describe at least four different birds and four different animals that live in your locality.
   D. Make a list of the poisonous plants and snakes in your area and how they can be identified.
   E. Tell what to do if you are lost.

II. First Aid
   A. Demonstrate how to stop bleeding.
   B. Demonstrate first aid for simple burns.
   C. Describe two important things to do when a person is seriously hurt.

III. Service
   Do a service for your church, such as clip hedge, mow lawn, etc.

IV. Bible
   A. Read Acts 2:1-4, Acts 8:14-17, Acts 10:44-46, Acts 19:1-6.
   B. Explain what is meant by the baptism in the Holy Spirit.

V. Your Church
   A. Draw a map showing the location of your church and your home, and describe how you would tell a person to find your church.

    B. Keep a record, by taking notes, of at least four of your pastor's sermons, giving Scripture references and main points of the sermon.
    C. Attend Sunday school regularly for six months.
VI. Your Home
    Show how you share in the responsibility of the home by making a list of the chores and errands you do.
VII. Your Outpost
    A. Lead your outpost in three games or activities.
    B. Lead in an outpost devotion.
VIII. Physical Fitness
    A. List two habits that harm our bodies and explain why.
    B. Explain why a balanced diet is needed for a healthy body.
    C. Do a regular physical exercise every day for six weeks such as push-ups, sit-ups, etc.
IX. Explain how you have lived by the Royal Ranger Code.
X. Carry Second Class Rank for at least six months.

Please note: All four advancement pins may be worn on the uniform at the same time. As new pins are earned, wear them on the uniform $\frac{1}{2}$ inch above the existing pin or pins.

ADVANCED RATING REQUIREMENTS

I. Campcraft
   A. Explain how to dress properly to go on a hike.
   B. Explain how to hike safely on the open road.
   C. Go on a hike of at least one mile.
   D. Cook a complete meal on a campfire.
   E. Demonstrate proper disposal of garbage.
   F. Demonstrate how to tie three different knots.
   G. Show how to find the direction north, using the stars and the sun.
   H. Describe at least six different birds and six different animals that live in your locality; also, identify four kinds of trees.

II. First Aid
   A. Demonstrate first aid for insect bites.
   B. Demonstrate first aid for sprained ankle.
   C. Demonstrate first aid for shock and fainting.
   D. Explain under what circumstances a person should not be moved.

III. The Bible
   A. Read the Book of Acts. Each time you read where someone was filled with the Spirit, underline it in your Bible.

B. Trace Paul's three missionary trips across land and sea on a map.

C. Describe which experience in Paul's life you enjoyed most.

IV. Service

Help publicize in your community two special events to be held at your church—such as revivals or vacation Bible schools—by passing out handbills or posters.

V. Your Church

A. Read the statements of fundamental beliefs of the Assemblies of God and ask your parents or pastor to assist you in explaining them. Then make a list of the things we believe.

B. Attend Sunday school regularly for six months after receiving First Class rating.

VI. Your Home

Explain what the Bible teaches about obeying our parents. Give a scripture reference.

VII. Your Outpost

Explain your outpost organization, giving the name of each officer.

VIII. Royal Ranger Code

Explain, by giving examples, how you have lived by four points of the Royal Ranger Code.

IX. Carry First Class rating six months.

MASTER RATING REQUIREMENTS

I. Campcraft
   A. Show that you know how to select and pack equipment for a one-night camp.
   B. Go on a one-night camp with your outpost.
   C. Help pitch a tent.
   D. Cook a complete meal on a campfire using two types of cooking: boiling, baking, broiling, or frying.
   E. Demonstrate how to sight and set a compass. Show how to lay out a course with a compass.
   F. Demonstrate how to play two outdoor games.
   G. Collect and identify leaves from five kinds of trees.
   Collect and identify a sample of three kinds of wood.
   In the field, identify three kinds of birds or animals making notes on how you were able to identify them.
   H. Be able to locate the Big Dipper, Little Dipper, and the North Star.

II. First Aid
   A. Demonstrate artificial respiration.
   B. Demonstrate first aid for arterial bleeding of arm or leg.
   C. Demonstrate first aid for blister on heel.
   D. Demonstrate first aid for skin poisoning from poison plants.

E. Demonstrate first aid for puncture wounds from nails, splinters, etc.
   F. Assemble a first-aid kit with all necessary items.
III. The Bible
   A. Read the Gospel of John.
      1. Read several verses a day until you complete the book.
      2. Each time you read the word "believe" underline it in your Bible.
   B. Read the following Scripture references: John 3:16; Romans 6:23; Luke 13:3; Romans 3:23; Acts 16:31. Decide what verse you would use to answer the following questions and write it in the blank following each question.
      1. How do I know I have sinned? _____

      2. Shall I be punished for my sins? _____

      3. Who died to save me from my sins?

      4. Must I repent of my sins to be saved?

      5. Must I trust Jesus to be saved? _____

IV. Service
   Learn how to be able to tell an unsaved friend how to be saved.

V. Your Church
   A. Give a talk before your outpost on the subject "What My Church Believes." Or write an article of at least 200 words on the same subject. Interview your pastor and secure his help in your presentation.
   B. Attend Sunday school regularly for at least six months after receiving Advanced Rating.
VI. Your Home
   Explain the importance of obedience to family rules in regard to permission to do things, go places, and when to return home.
VII. Your Outpost
   Assist in the outpost leadership by helping other boys in advancement or serve as a Guide or Assistant Guide.
VIII. Royal Ranger Code
   Give a brief talk before the Outpost Council on the subject, "The Importance of Living by the Royal Ranger Code."
IX. Carry Advanced Rating six months.

Boys who have earned Master Rating in the Pioneers are permitted to earn the Advanced Awards listed in the *Trailblazer Handbook*. These awards are worn over the left pocket directly under the Pioneer Advancement Pins.

PIONEERING IN
THE OUT-OF-DOORS

HIKING
There is nothing like the adventure of hiking along wilderness trails that were worn down by moccasined feet in pioneer days, or along leaf-covered paths in the forest, with the sound of birds filling the air, or along mountain trails with new discoveries at every turn.

CAMPING
There is nothing like the experience of getting out-of-doors, finding a good camping spot by a stream, pitching your tent, building a campfire and cooking your meals over it, sitting around a council fire at night singing songs and telling stories, lying in your sleeping bag listening to the sound of night birds and animals, getting up at dawn and filling your lungs with good, clean morning air, and doing all the other enjoyable things that go along with camping.

CAMPCRAFT

Since you like outdoor adventure, camping and hiking have been placed high on the list of activities for Royal Rangers. To enjoy these experiences a Pioneer should learn to take care of himself in the out-of-doors safely and comfortably. For this reason he should learn skills in ropecraft, sanitation, shelter and equipment, firecraft, and cooking.

These skills are not listed in this handbook, but are described in the Royal Rangers' campbook entitled *Adventures in Camping*. You should purchase this book and learn all the camping skills. Then when the time comes to go on a hike or a camping trip, you will be ready to enjoy it completely.

NATURE STUDY

Everyone should become better acquainted with nature. Making new discoveries about animals, birds, fish, trees, and stars through nature study is the Royal Ranger way of learning more about

God's world. To catch the quick flash of a deer's tail as it disappears in the woods; to see the beaver before it dives off into its dam, a lizard disappear under a rock, a hawk soaring high into the sky, the flash of blue as a kingfisher dives for a minnow; or to hear the whistle of a woodchuck, the far-away hoot of an owl, the chatter of a squirrel, the song of a mockingbird—all these are the rewards of the student of nature.

Just as every Royal Ranger has a community in which he lives, so has every animal, insect, fish, reptile, or bird. Those who study nature call these communities "habitats." Almost all of nature's creatures would fit in one of the following habitats or communities: (1) water, (2) marshes or swamps, (3) grasslands or prairies, (4) forest or woods, (5) deserts, (6) mountaintops. Wherever a Royal Ranger lives, one of these habitats is nearby. Each one is filled with interesting things to discover.

For further information, obtain from your library "The Golden Nature Study Series" or any good encyclopedia. There are also many other good books available on nature study in your library.

PIONEERING IN
FIRST AID

"... And went to him and bound up his wounds" (Luke 10:34).

Send or Go for a Doctor

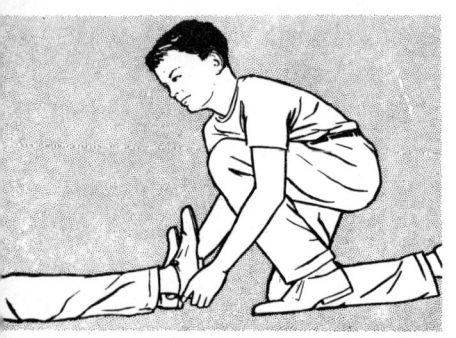

Give Needed First Aid

First aid is the immediate care given to anyone who is badly hurt. The word "first" suggests that more aid is to follow—the aid given by a doctor. Therefore, first aid is the temporary aid you give someone before the doctor arrives. It is also the immediate care given to slight injuries to prevent them from becoming more serious.

Things to do when giving first aid to someone seriously hurt or seriously ill include the following. FIRST, send for a doctor. SECOND, make the patient as comfortable as possible. Do not move a person if there is reason to believe there is serious head injury or broken bones (unless bones are properly splinted). THIRD, give necessary first aid to the patient. FOURTH, be calm and cheerful. Your patient is probably scared and suffering from shock. If you can do your job calmly and meet his anxiety with a smile and words of assurance, you will help him a lot.

FIRST-AID KITS

A first-aid kit is a necessity for each outpost. Having on hand the things you need when you need them is as important as knowing how to treat a wound.

Any type of box will do to hold first-aid supplies. The box should be sturdy and well marked. Each boy should know where the kit is located.

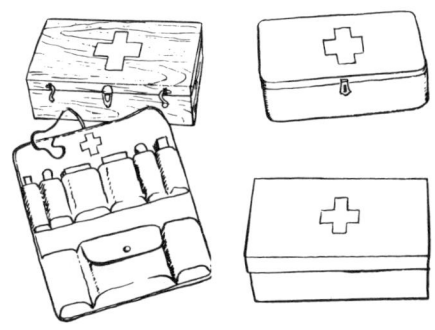

The following items should be included in an outpost first-aid kit. First, a roll or two of 1-inch or wider gauze bandage. Place a gauze pad on wound and spiral wind the bandage around it.

Two- to four-inch gauze pads are handy for larger wounds. Place on wound and wind bandage around it.

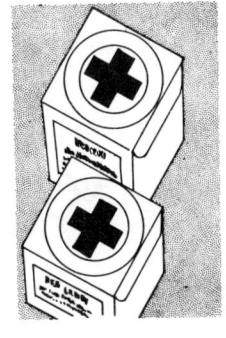 

Triangular bandages are useful as an emergency cover, arm sling, dressing, and for other purposes.

Ammonia ampules will revive a person who has fainted.

Calamine lotion is good for insect bites or stings.

Rubbing alcohol is good for sponging skin exposed to poison ivy.

If your drinking water is not guaranteed to be pure, boil it. Next, treat it with a purifier, halazone tablets, or liquid chlorine laundry bleach. When using chlorine, for example, apply two drops of bleach to 1 quart of water. Mix thoroughly and let stand for 30 minutes before drinking.

One- or two-inch adhesive tape has many uses in first-aid work.

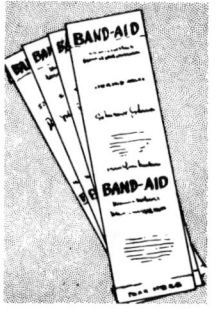

A bar of soap should be used to wash wounds.

Band-aids are good to use on small cuts or wounds.

SIMPLE WOUNDS

Wash a small wound with soap and water. Dry the skin and cover the wound with a band-aid.

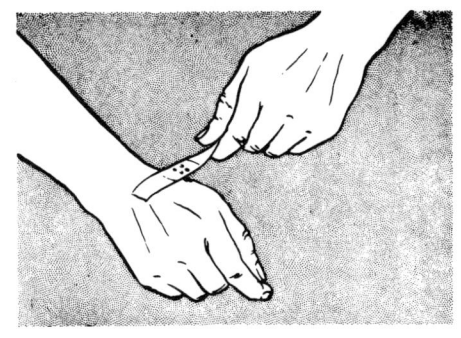

LARGE WOUNDS

Cover a large wound with a sterile compress and wrap with bandage. Use a square knot to tie end of bandage.

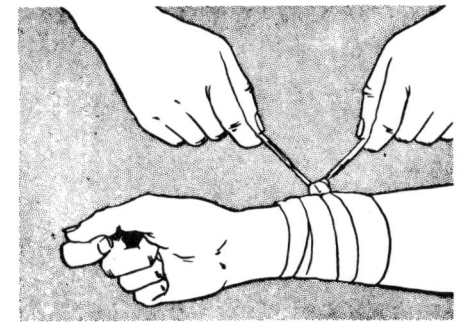

SPLINTERS

Use a pair of tweezers to pull a splinter from under the skin. Then work antiseptic well into the wound.

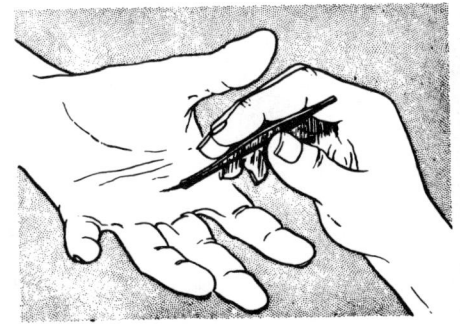

SIMPLE BURNS

Flush or submerge the injured part in cold water. Apply a dry dressing if it is necessary.

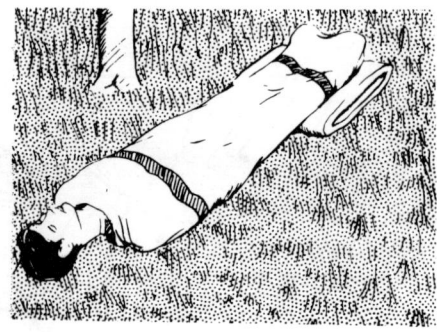

SHOCK

Where there is an accident, there may be shock! Lay the person down. Keep him warm. Place something under the feet. If the person is having breathing difficulty, lower the feet and elevate the head and shoulders.

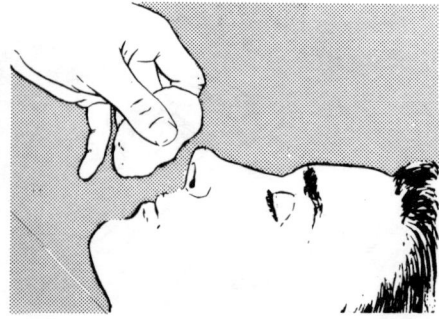

FAINTING

When a person faints, lay him down with the feet raised higher than the head. Pour a few drops of aromatic spirits of ammonia on cotton cloth and place it near the nose.

NOSEBLEED

For nosebleed, bend the head forward. Place a cold compress over the nose. Press the nostrils together.

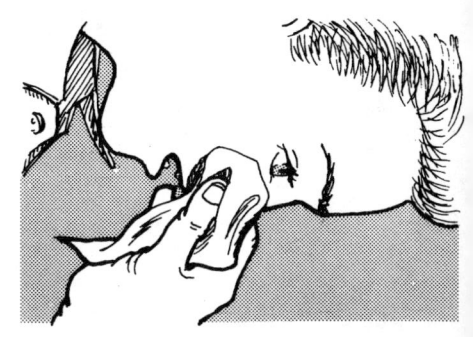

BLACK EYE

A black eye is a bruise. A cold compress will relieve pain and prevent swelling.

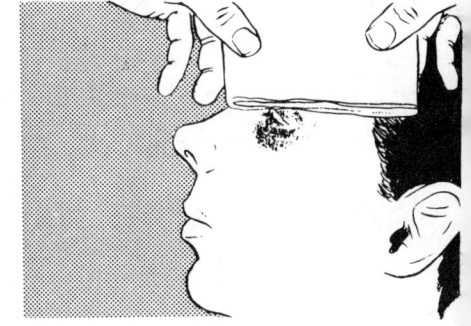

Improvised Blanket Stretcher

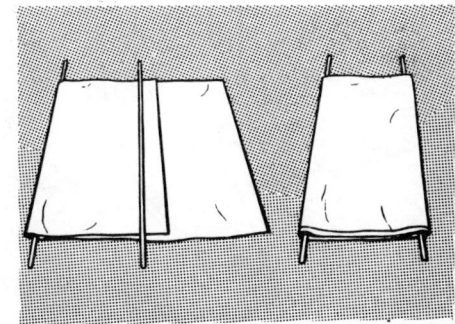

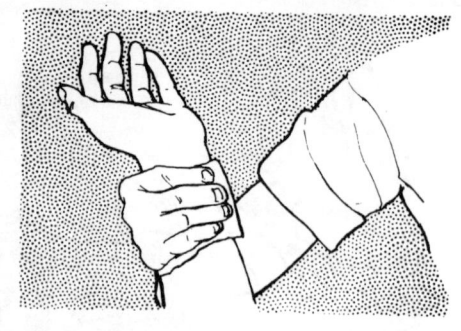

BLEEDING

Apply direct pressure to wound and elevate the injured part. You can do this best by placing the cleanest material available against the bleeding point. Apply pressure with your hand until a bandage can be applied. Most wounds can be cared for in this manner.

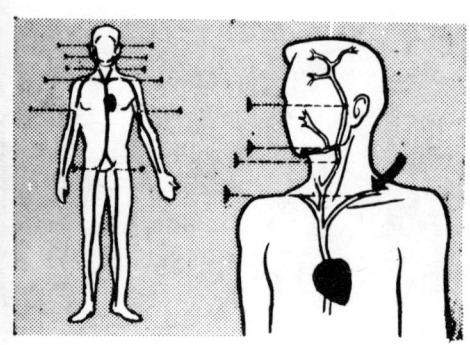

ARTERIAL BLEEDING

When a deep gash spurts blood from a cut artery or larger veins, it is like a break in a water pipe. We shut off the flow by pressure nearest the pump—the heart. Know the pressure points shown in the diagram.

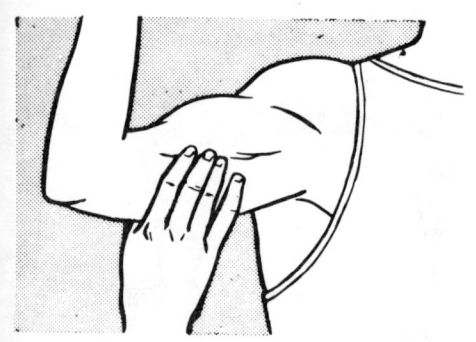

APPLYING PRESSURE

At each point the artery passes over a bone. When you press your hand against the bone, you flatten out the artery just like pinching a rubber tube to stop the flow of water. When the blood stops, it means you have the right spot.

SPRAINS

Sprains are injuries to the soft tissues surrounding joints. The ankles, fingers, wrists, and knees are most often affected. Ankle sprains commonly result when weight is thrown forcefully upon a turned ankle. Apply cold wet application or ice bag during the first half-hour to retard swelling. Keep the joint elevated. Do not walk on sprain until it has protective support.

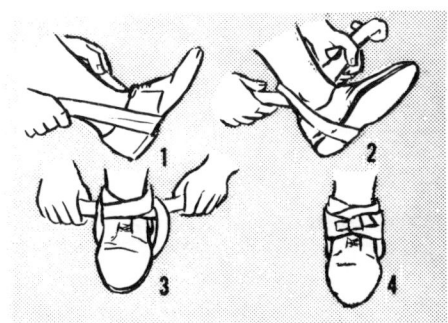

BLISTERS ON HEEL

Do your best to prevent blisters. If you do get one, wash it with soap and water or clear water. Cover it with sterile dressing and adhesive tape. If the blister has been broken, treat it like any other wound. A blister should not be opened except by a doctor. Foot injuries are dangerous and should not be neglected.

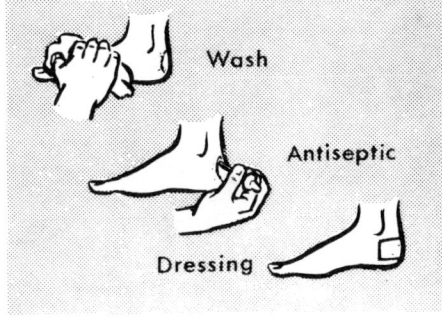

POISON PLANTS

If you have been in contact with poison ivy, poison oak, or poison sumac, wash the exposed area with strong soap and water; then sponge it with rubbing alcohol. Apply calamine lotion to relieve itching, or you may make a solution of baking soda or Epsom salts and apply to the infected area.

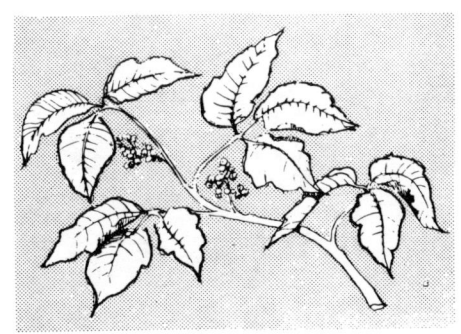

ARTIFICIAL RESPIRATION

Mouth-to-Mouth Method

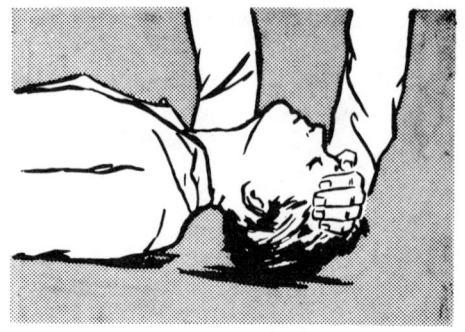

1. If there is foreign matter visible in the mouth, wipe it out quickly with your fingers or a cloth wrapped around your fingers.

2. Tilt the head back so the chin is pointing upward.

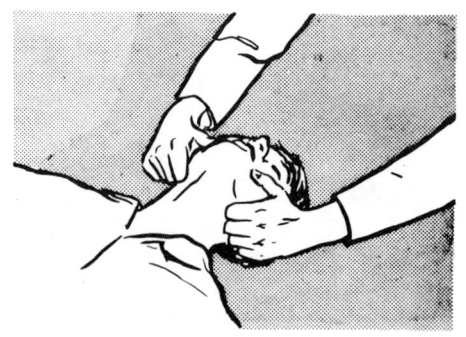

3. Pull or push the jaw into a jutting-out position.

4. Open your mouth wide and place it tightly over victim's mouth. At same time pinch victim's nostrils shut.

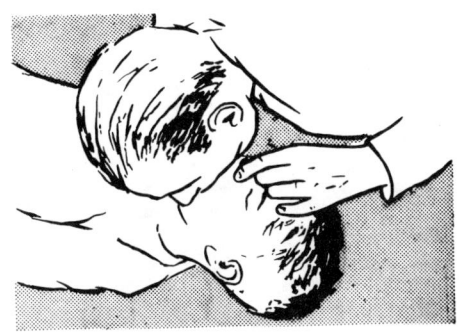

5. Or close the nostrils with your cheek. Or close the victim's mouth and place your mouth over the nose.

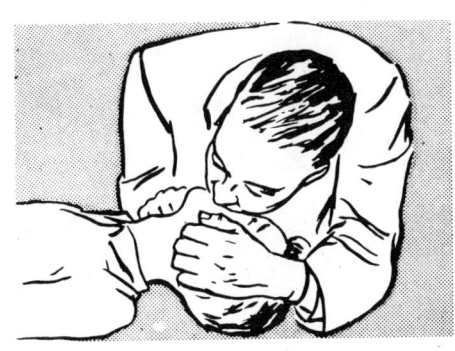

6. Blow into the victim's mouth or nose. If you are not getting air exchange, recheck the head and jaw position.

PIONEERING IN
PHYSICAL FITNESS

The person who is physically fit has a great deal of what sports writers call "bounce." His body has the power to recover promptly from minor bruises to his tissues or his personality. Physical fitness should be practiced throughout life. This means enough sleep, right kind of food, regular exercise, rest periods, cleanliness, and recreation.

SLEEP

When you work or play hard you get tired. During sleep, the mind becomes quiet except for dreams, muscles relax, and the heart beats fewer times per minute, and breathing becomes slower. Therefore, sleep brings rest and gives us strength for a new day.

How much sleep do you usually get? Do you have a rest period during the day? Do you find time to play some active games each day?

These are important questions for you to think about, because sleep, rest, and play are necessary if you expect to be healthy and grow strong. Boys your age should have 10 to 11 hours sleep each night. You need to play some enjoyable running games. At the same time it is important that you have periods of rest so you will not become too tired. Plan your day so that you will have enough sleep, rest, and play.

FOOD

Every boy likes to eat just to be eating. But there are reasons other than because we enjoy it. Really we have four basic needs for food. The first is for *building material*. The body needs food to build all its parts. The second need is for material *to repair and replace* wornout cells or tissues. The third is to *supply* the body with *heat and energy*. The fourth need is to help the different parts of the body *work properly*. Many different kinds of foods are needed to accomplish all this. Do you eat several kinds of foods that will give your body all that it needs?

Something to Do: Talk with your mother or health teacher about why we eat. Discuss with them the need for several kinds of foods. Then use the chart to keep a record of different kinds of foods you eat and right amounts of food.

Kinds of Foods	Daily Amount	M	T	W	T	F	S	S
Milk & milk products [1]	1 quart							
Eggs	1							
Potatoes [2]	1 serving							
Meat	1 serving (at least)							
Cereals [3]	1 serving							
Butter or Margarine [4]	2 servings (at least)							
Fruits [5]	2 or more servings							
Vegetables [6]	1 serving (at least)							

1. Some of it may be in the form of ice cream, cream soup, or cheese.
2. Either Irish or sweet potato.
3. At least two slices of whole-grain or enriched bread in addition to cereal.
4. Margarine should be fortified (vitamin A added).
5. One should be a citrus fruit or tomato.
6. At least two different kinds beside potato. One should be raw. One should be green or yellow.

EXERCISE

"Okay men," cried Coach Hardy, "let's warm up!" The football players of Central High had assembled before the coach and were ready to begin their "warm up" exercises. Early in the season Coach Hardy had explained to the squad members the importance of exercise. He had pointed out that the right kind and proper amount of exercise would help them become stronger and more healthy.

Every growing boy needs plenty of exercise. It is important to have a "warm up" period before heavy exercise so that muscles will gradually get used to hard work.

It should be remembered that among the main reasons for recreational exercise are the benefits of sunshine and air. Walking, swimming, tennis, etc., are some very good outdoor exercises.

Something to Do: Talk with a doctor or an athletic coach about the importance of exercise. Then answer the test below. If the statement is true, circle "T"; if it is false, circle "F."

1. T F   Exercise helps make muscles strong.
2. T F   It is good to take as much as possible of your exercise indoors.
3. T F   Exercise helps develop good posture.
4. T F   The digestion of food is aided by proper exercise.
5. T F   Exercise makes the heart beat faster and harder, which helps the blood do its work better.

PERSONAL CARE

Cleanliness is a must. A boy should take a cleansing bath with soap and warm water daily. The face and hands should be washed more often. The hair should be brushed twice a day. Oily hair should be washed once a week. Dry hair may not have to be washed more than once every two weeks. The teeth should be brushed by brushing from the gums to the teeth within thirty minutes after every meal. If a brush is not convenient, rinse the mouth well with water to neutralize the sugar around the teeth. Cutting down on candy, pastries, sweet drinks, and sugar-coated gum will help to check dental decay. A clean mouth adds to good health.

POISON—BEWARE!

Wise people don't take something they know to be poisonous, do they? Yet millions of people take poison into their bodies every day by smoking. One is nicotine, which is used as a spray to kill harmful insects. Most athletic coaches have strict rules against smoking by players. They know their players will not have the endurance and strength to do their best if they smoke. In many ways tobacco is harmful to growing boys. Many doctors believe smoking is the main cause of lung cancer.

Something to Do: Arrange an interview with an athletic coach. Discuss with him the training rules of his team members. Is smoking permitted? Why? Answer the test below. If the statement is true, circle "T"; if it is false, circle "F."

1. T F Some famous athletes endorse certain brands of cigarettes, so smoking cannot be harmful.

2. T F It is all right to smoke once in a while because it is easy to stop.
3. T F Smoking has no effect on one's appetite for proper foods.
4. T F To make friends and be grown-up, you must smoke.
5. T F Smoking is an expensive habit.

VENTILATION

Fresh air is important to health. Usually we don't have any trouble getting plenty of it out of doors, but often rooms are not well ventilated. A well-ventilated room is one in which the warm, "used up" air passes slowly out of the room while the fresh, outdoor air comes slowly in. Opening the windows (to suit the weather) at the top and bottom in your bedroom is one way of getting a circulation of air. Usually a sign of a well-ventilated room is one with a temperature of about 72 degrees.

Is your bedroom well ventilated? Check and see.

Something to Do: Hang a thermometer in your bedroom. Check the temperature at bedtime for a week, and record it on the chart below.

DAY	DEGREES
Monday	
Tuesday	
Wednesday	
Thursday	
Friday	
Saturday	
Sunday	

PIONEERING IN
YOUR OUTPOST

The activities of your outpost will open to you new doors to fun, adventure, and friendship. To better enjoy the great time you will be having with a swell bunch of fellows, you should understand the way your outpost is set up. Also, you should become acquainted with each officer of the outpost and his duties.

YOUR OUTPOST COUNCIL

The Outpost Council is a group of from three to five men who direct the Royal Ranger program in the church. They are responsible for the appointing of the Outpost Commander and Assistant Commander. Also, they arrange a meeting place for each outpost and obtain needed equipment for activities and projects.

When the fellows have passed the requirements for an advancement in rank, the Outpost Council will set up a special presentation service and present them with their awards.

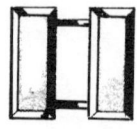 

SENIOR COMMANDER

When churches have more than one Royal Ranger outpost, a Senior Commander may be appointed to coordinate the overall Royal Ranger program in the church. He supports the Outpost Commanders in carrying out their responsibilities and serves in an advisory role.

YOUR OUTPOST COMMANDER

The Outpost Commander directs the activities of the outpost such as outpost meetings, camping trips, hikes, etc. He is trained to assist the Royal Rangers in their advancement in rank and will determine when they pass each requirement.

LIEUTENANT COMMANDER

The Lieutenant Commander has the responsibility of assisting the Outpost Commander in the activities of the outpost. At each meeting he directs certain activities—such as games, crafts, etc. Should the Commander be absent, he assumes charge of the meeting or outing.

JUNIOR COMMANDER

A Junior Commander is appointed to assist the Commander and Lieutenant Commander in the various activities of the outpost. He should be prepared to lead in games, crafts, and other outpost recreational activities at the request of the Commander or Lieutenant Commander. He should be ready to assist other members of the outpost in advancement. The final approval of the advancement requirement should be made by the Commander; however, preliminary grading and reviewing by the Junior Commander can be very helpful to the Commander as well as to the boy applying for advancement.

During campouts he should be prepared to assist in setting up camp, judging contests, supervising recreation, teaching campcraft classes, conducting council fires, and other camp-related activities. The Commander will decide which of these areas the Junior Commander will supervise. In some cases the Junior Commander may be requested to assist in outpost or campfire devotions.

The Junior Commander should also be willing to assist in recruiting new members for the outpost and in visiting and encouraging old members who may have dropped out of the outpost.

The role of the Junior Commander is basically that of *assisting*. He should not assume full responsibility for an outpost meeting or campout.

 SENIOR GUIDE

The Senior Guide should carry at least a First-Class rating. (If the outpost is new, a Senior Guide may be temporarily appointed without this rank.) His term of office shall be six months, and he should serve no longer than one year at any one time.

The Senior Guide is a Royal Ranger appointed by the Commander to coordinate the activities of the patrols. He serves as a liaison leader between the patrols and the Commander. During outpost meetings he calls the roll and keeps records of each meeting, using the *Outpost Record Book*. He may also assist in recreation, meeting features, premeeting activities, opening ceremonies, and closing ceremonies at the request of the Commander.

His major role is to encourage the patrol leaders in carrying out their duties and to evaluate each of the patrols to see if they are measuring up to the standards of the outpost. During the campouts he double-checks to see if each patrol has set up camp properly. He then follows through to see if each patrol is following proper camp routine, such as cooking, safety, sanitation, and rest; and he makes sure each patrol is attending each function during the campout.

He may also be requested by the Commander to assist in other camp-related activities, such as judging contests, recreation, and special projects. He also conducts stunt time during the council fire and gives appropriate applause after each stunt.

Because of his vital role in the outpost he endeavors to be the very best example of the high standards of Royal Rangers.

PATROL GUIDE

The Patrol Guide should carry at least a Second Class rating. (If the outpost is new, a Guide may be temporarily elected without this rank.) His term of office shall be six months, and he should serve no longer than one year at any one time.

The Patrol Guide is elected by his own patrol. He is basically responsible for leading his patrol in all patrol-related activities. If his patrol does not have a name, a flag, a song, and a yell he is responsible for encouraging his patrol to develop these items. If his patrol is given a project or duty, he is responsible for seeing that these assignments are carried out. During outpost meetings or outdoor assemblies he reports for his patrol. During campouts his patrol may be assigned as the Duty Patrol. He should therefore be prepared to lead his patrol in the presentation of colors.

He should become completely familiar with his patrol's role and position in all outpost formations, outpost assemblies, and special ceremonies.

During campouts, his patrol will be camping as a patrol. He should therefore supervise all camp-related patrol activities. These areas include setting up the campsite, food preparation, sanitation, duty assignments, recreation, and overall participation in the campout program. He makes sure each patrol member performs the tasks assigned to him on the patrol duty roster. He is also required to carry his patrol flag with him from the campsite to all official functions. When marching with his patrol he will march at the head of the column.

Because of his important role, the Patrol Guide should also endeavor to be the best example of what a Royal Ranger should be.

ASSISTANT PATROL GUIDE

The Assistant Patrol Guide is also elected by his own patrol. His title clearly describes his role. He is to *assist* the Patrol Guide in carrying out his responsibilities. In the absence of the Guide at either outpost meetings or during outdoor activities, the Assistant Guide will assume his position until he returns. When marching with his patrol, the Assistant Guide will march at the rear of the column.

Because his responsibilities are also very important, the Assistant Guide, too, should always endeavor to be the best example of what a Royal Ranger should be.

OUTPOST STAFF

The Outpost Staff is composed of the Commander, Assistant Commanders, Senior Guide, and Patrol Guides. The staff meets at different times to discuss plans for outpost meetings, projects, and other activities.

PATROLS

The patrol is a special gang of fellows that do things together within the Royal Rangers program. Each outpost is divided into two or more patrols. The boys of each patrol will select a name in keeping with the ideals of Royal Rangers and elect its own Guide and Assistant Guide. Each week, during the outpost meeting, time is set aside for patrols to meet. Games will be played between patrols during game periods, and each patrol will sit or stand together during ceremonies.

OUTPOST FORMATION

The Commander stands facing the outpost with his Lieutenant Commanders beside him. The Senior Guide is in front of the Commander. When in charge or calling roll, the Senior Guide faces the outpost; he faces the Commander when he is reporting or when the Commander is in charge.

The Guide always stands at the right end of his patrol formation. The Assistant Guide stands at the left end of each patrol line.

This formation is for the purpose of opening ceremonies, roll call, closing ceremonies, etc.

PATROL REPORTING

The proper way for a Patrol Guide to report to the Senior Guide during outpost meetings or morning assemblies during campouts is as follows:

The Patrol Guide will come to attention holding his patrol flag in his left hand. He will salute with his right hand and state, while holding the salute, "Eagle Patrol (or proper patrol name), all present and accounted for, Sir." He will then drop his hand salute. If all the patrols are not present, he might state, for example, "Eagle Patrol has 6 members present and 2 absent." During outpost meetings the Patrol Guide would simply stand up and report. However, during outdoor assemblies he would take one step forward to report.

OUTPOST FORMATIONS

LT. COMMANDER   COMMANDER   LT. COMMANDER

SENIOR GUIDE

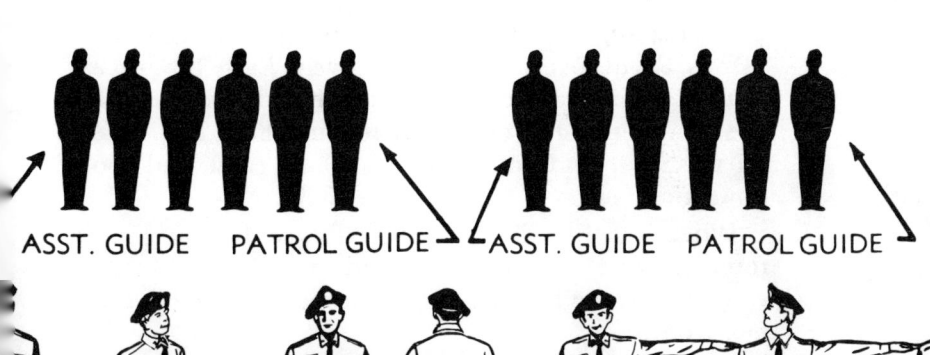

ASST. GUIDE   PATROL GUIDE   ASST. GUIDE   PATROL GUIDE

AT EASE   PARADE REST   DRESS RIGHT DRESS

"COMMANDS" DURING OUTPOST FORMATIONS

At the command "Attention" the Royal Ranger brings his heels together and stands with shoulders back, eyes front, chin up, arms at the sides, each thumb at the trousers' seam. Toes are pointed outward at an angle of 45 degrees.

At the command "At Ease" the Royal Ranger can relax but is not to talk. "At Rest" permits him to talk. In either case one foot is to be kept in place.

At the command "Parade Rest" the left foot is to be moved 12 inches to the left and the right hand clasped with the left behind the back.

On "Fall Out" Rangers may leave their position in formation, but must stay nearby to resume their places at the command "Fall In."

In forming the unit after "Fall In," the command "Dress Right Dress" is usually given. Each boy except at the left end of the line extends his arm and touches the shoulder of the man next to him. Each boy except on the right end turns his head half right and looks down the line.

When the line is straight and each boy at proper interval, the Commander orders "Ready Front"; whereupon, the boys drop their arms to their sides and face front.

To dismiss a formation the command "Dismissed" is given.

WORKING TOGETHER

Bridges are interesting structures, aren't they? One of the most famous bridges in our country is the Golden Gate Bridge which connects northern California to the peninsula of San Francisco. This type of bridge is known as a suspension bridge because it is suspended or hung from two large steel cables.

Each of the cables is $36\frac{1}{2}$ inches thick. Can you imagine cables that large? To get an idea how big around each cable is, draw a circle with a radius of 18 inches. (Ask your dad to help you measure and draw the circle.)

What a cable! But the interesting thing about the cable is that it is made up of hundreds and hundreds of strands of wire. By twisting these single strands of wire together, two giant cables strong enough to support the great Golden Gate Bridge were made.

Separately, the strands of wire have very little strength. Together, they support a bridge more than a mile long.

You and your Pioneer outpost work something like this. Your outpost is made up of several boys. This makes it possible for you and the other fellows to work together. Just as the strands of wire work together to hold the great bridge, Pioneers work together in their outpost to serve Christ.

If just one strand of wire should break, the cable would become weakened. If just one Pioneer fails in his responsibilities, his outpost is weakened. So it is important that you and other outpost members be as strong members as possible.

You can do this by attending meetings regularly, reading your handbook, and taking part in all of your outpost activities. By doing so you will be strengthening the work of your outpost as it tries to serve others.

THE PATROL SYSTEM

Your Royal Rangers outpost is built on the patrol system. You probably were already introduced to the members of your patrol and your patrol guide when you joined the group. In fact, you were probably invited to the meeting by a member of the patrol—one of your friends. And now you are a patrol member.

It's a big, exciting responsibility to be a patrol member. And you probably have a million questions—like "What is a patrol anyway?" And, "What does a patrol do?" "What's a patrol guide?" And, "How do I fit in?" Well, let's see if we can answer some of these.

YOUR PATROL

A patrol is a special gang of friends that do things together in the outpost. A patrol may have as many as eight Rangers, or as few as four. They have a special name like the Screaming Eagles or the Snarling Panthers, and a patrol call or yell that goes along with it. They have a patrol standard or flag that carries their emblem on it, along with the names of their members. In most outposts, they meet every week during regular outpost meetings. These little meetings are called "Patrol Corners." During this time, you and the other patrol members will work on different things—advancements, patrol equipment, upcoming outpost and patrol events, and other exciting projects.

In some outposts, your patrol will also get the opportunity to meet outside of the regular patrol meetings at one of the members' homes. During these meetings you will do more of the things that you do during the Patrol Corners time. You will learn more about Royal Rangers and the skills that you need to become the best Ranger in the outpost.

On outpost camp-outs, you will camp with the other members of your patrol. Your patrol will set up its own tents, cook its own food, and sometimes even work on important patrol projects. You will build lasting friendships in your patrol—ones that will never be forgotten. You will take pride in the things that you and your friends accomplish by working together.

And that really captures the essence of what a patrol is: you and your friends, other patrol members, working together to make your patrol and outpost number one. Everybody pulling together—that's what a patrol is!

YOUR PATROL AT WORK

In order for your patrol to do all these terrific things, you need some sort of method to follow, some way to organize that will let each of you contribute his "fair share." This method is called the patrol system, and using it will help each of you do your best to become the best patrol in the outpost.

The patrol system starts with your patrol guide. He's one of the patrol members that you elect to lead the patrol. Your guide, along with the other guides in your outpost, and the senior guide, will make up the Gold Bar Staff. This group will help run the outpost. They will make recommendations for camp-outs, activities—in short, they will help decide what the outpost will do.

Your guide should hold at least a second-class rating. He should show that he is willing to not only lead, but also represent you and the other members of your patrol at the Gold Bar Staff Meetings. Take care in selecting him. In most outposts, you and your friends will get to elect your own patrol guide. Don't make the election a popularity contest, but elect a guide that you feel will do a good job. A good guide will represent your views whether or not he agrees with them, and whether or not they are the majority's views. That's the kind of guide you want for your patrol. Choose him carefully.

The patrol will choose an assistant guide to help the guide with his duties and to fill in for him in his absence. Like your guide, he will work hard for your patrol and your interests. Be sure to give him your help and respect.

As we said before, your patrol guide and the other patrol guides in your outpost will make up the Gold Bar Staff. At the Gold Bar Staff meetings, the senior guide, with some help from the outpost commander, will work with the guides to suggest plans for the entire outpost program. They will take your ideas, and the ideas of others in the patrol and outpost, and put together the kind of activities that will make your outpost grow. Your guide will know what you want done by talking to you during the Patrol Corners and patrol meetings. Be sure to be present at each meeting—you never know what you might miss!

YOUR PATROL SPIRIT

Patrol spirit is a mysterious kind of thing—sort of like oxygen. You can't see oxygen, but you can sure tell when it's missing—everything dies! It's the same with patrol spirit. You really can't tell what it is, but you can tell when it isn't there. The patrol without it has no spark, no enthusiasm, no drive.

Patrol spirit is the "something" that makes every patrol member want to give his best—no matter what the goal is, no matter where the patrol is headed or what they are doing. Patrol spirit turns patrol members from being "sunshine Rangers" into all-weather Rangers who turn out no matter what. It gives you pride in your patrol: pride to wear your uniform correctly to every meeting, pride to carry the patrol standard, pride to give the patrol call.

Patrol spirit might be defined as patrol pride. Not the swell-headed, bragging kind, but the confident kind. The kind that says we can do it!

To a large extent, patrol spirit depends on you. You can either feed it and watch it grow, or you can starve it and watch it die.

It's like a flame. Once a match is lit, that flame will keep burning as long as it has fuel. Keep feeding it and it will burn forever. If you put everything into all that your patrol does, if you show up for every meeting early and fully uniformed, if you work hard on every project, if you advance as quickly as you can, patrol spirit will grow.

On the other hand, if you fight every suggestion that comes up, if you stay home when your guide calls a patrol meeting, if you show up late and out of uniform and goof off on patrol outings and projects, you will pour cold water on the flame of patrol spirit. It will die—and die quickly.

So determine now that you are going to do everything you can to build patrol spirit. Invite new members to join your patrol. Learn your patrol's call and song. Work hard on patrol projects. Respect and help your guide and assistants. You will be proud of the results.

YOU, PATROL MEMBER

There you have it—a patrol. You and your friends working together, hiking and camping together, learning together, and heading toward one common goal: becoming the best Royal Rangers that you can be. It's a big responsibility; the other boys in your patrol are counting on you to do your share to build the patrol. It's hard. But then, everything that's important takes work. You can do it!

PATROL STANDARDS

These are very easy to make and are very inexpensive. Equipment needed is a stick or staff or any type of wood 5 feet long, a crosspiece of the same type of wood about 1 foot long, and a piece of board, leather, cloth, vinyl, or birch bark (10 x 14 inches in size) for making the standard. The standard should contain the name of the patrol (see illustration). The standard is secured to the crosspiece and to the staff with nails or tacks (see illustration). Other decorations and frills may be added if desired.

These standards are used at campsites to identify patrols, in the patrol corners of the outpost meeting room, and as banners during parades or hikes.

PATROL FLAG

A patrol flag is made in the same way as a standard, except the staff does not have a crosspiece. The flag is secured to one side of the staff and allowed to drape down.

The patrol flag does not display the name of the patrol as well as the standard because of the draping effect of the flag.

HOW TO MAKE A PATROL STANDARD

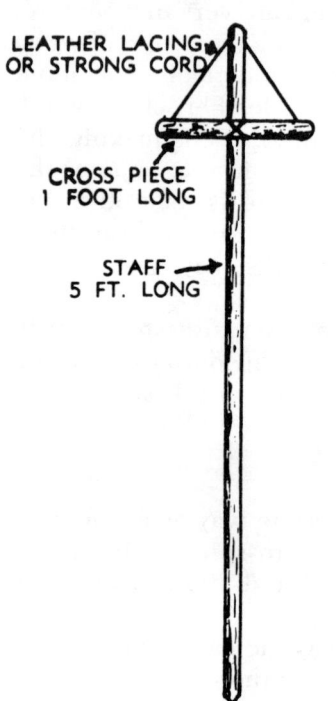

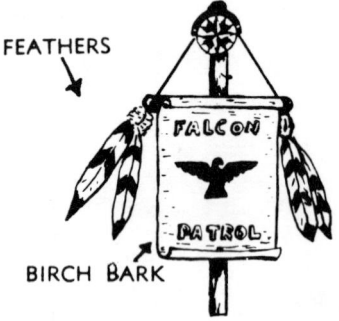

HOW TO MAKE BOLO SLIDES

Bolo ties may be worn as a part of the uniform instead of the dress tie during hot weather or on campouts. They should be worn loosely with the shirt collar open. Bolo ties are available from the Gospel Publishing House. However, the outpost may make their own bolo ties as a craft project; use small nylon rope or leather boot strings. We suggest that each patrol make a different type of bolo slide. This will help identify their patrol. There are almost unlimited possibilities for bolo slide designs. Those illustrated are only a few examples.

EXAMPLE OF BOLO SLIDES

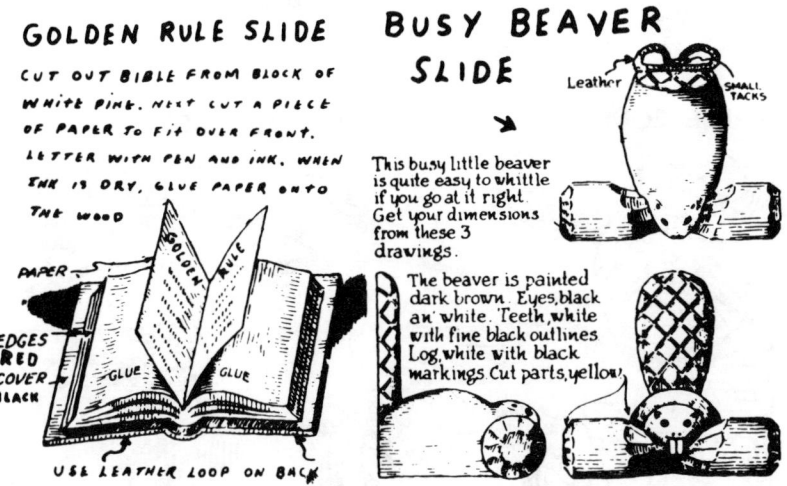

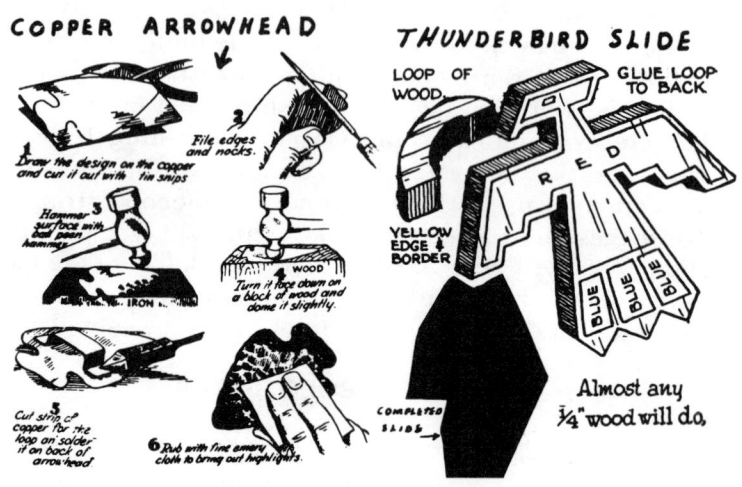

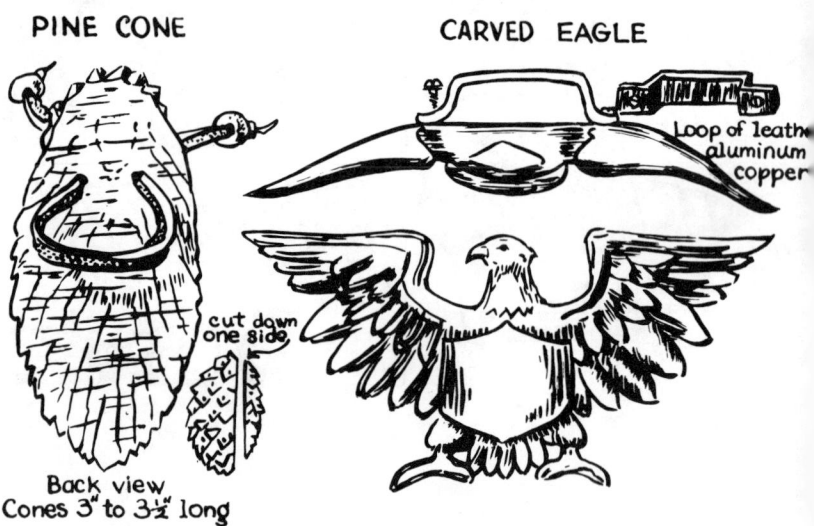

HOW TO MAKE AN AWARD VEST

An award vest is an ideal way for Royal Rangers to display a record of their achievements, ratings, Pow Wows, and Camporees. They may display advancement pins, chevrons, advanced awards, and Guide bars which they have previously received in any age division. Camporee and Pow Wow patches can also be displayed in this way.

These vests may be worn during any Royal Rangers activity, except formal occasions, such as banquets and church services.

Make the vest from buckskin, suede cloth, or felt and lace it with leather or plastic lacing. Punch holes for lacing with a sharp leather chisel or make a chisel from a nail with a file. Use an old vest as a pattern or secure a vest pattern from a store. This would make a good outpost craft project.

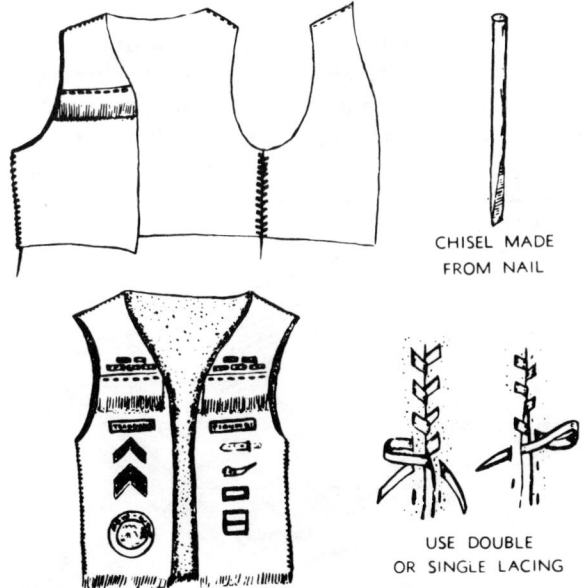

CHISEL MADE FROM NAIL

USE DOUBLE OR SINGLE LACING

PATROL NAME

The patrol should choose a name that represents the whole group. It should be in good taste, and a name the gang can be proud of. Perhaps it's an animal or bird. If you choose an animal or bird, it should be of a particular kind—something that has action, like a screaming eagle, a growling bear, or a busy beaver. Some other sources for patrol names are: nature names, Bible names, Indian names, historical names, pioneer names, or a name selected as a result of an experience the patrol shared. Plenty of time should be taken in selecting the name. All of the patrol should think about a proper name. When a name is selected, it should be included in the song and yell and be illustrated on the patrol standard or flag.

PATROL LOG

An ideal patrol project is making and keeping a patrol log or scrapbook. This log should contain such items as photos, sketches, patches, awards, or anything else that would display the activities and history of the patrol. The cover may be made from leather, wood, or other durable material. It should be bound in such a way that additional pages may be added later if needed.

PATROL SONGS AND YELLS

Nothing cultivates patrol spirit more than lively patrol songs and enthusiastic yells.

Consider the following in preparing a good patrol song:

1. Should be easy to sing. Most patrols will select the tune of a familiar song and change the words to fit their patrol.

2. Should have the patrol name included in the words of the song.

3. Should have somewhat of a marching beat so it can be sung while marching on the trail as well as in an outpost meeting.

A yell is a short phrase used by a patrol, which allows them to "put everything into it" by yelling at the top of their voices. It should be brief and also incorporate the name of the patrol. Here is an example: "Some are short, some are tall—but the Fox Patrol is the best of all! Yea—!"

PIONEERING IN
GOD'S WORD

THE BIBLE

God's Word is filled with adventure and excitement. The Bible is the record of how God tells men about Himself and His plan.

The Bible is a collection of 66 books written by men of several races, during different periods of time, and at different places. Yet God speaks clearly through each of them. The Bible contains history, stories, poems, riddles, biographies, plays, letters, sermons, and laws.

Some books are called "the year's best seller" because they outsell all other books. More copies of the Bible have been sold than of any other book.

Most important, this book tells about God, who made all life. Through the pages of the Bible, we read about the greatness of God's love for all people through the death and resurrection of Jesus Christ the Saviour.

The Bible gives the message of salvation—explaining what people, the world over, must do to be saved.

In the following pages are a few of the many interesting stories in the Bible.

GOD, THE CREATOR

Two boys were arguing one day about how old the world is. Bob declared emphatically, "The earth is just millions of years old! I read that it is." Walter disagreed with him. "I know it's not," Walter said. "It's only six thousand years old."

Just then their friend George walked up, and Bob asked him what he thought about it. George thought a minute. Then he said, "I don't know how old the world is, but I know God made it. That is what's really important."

George was right. A person can learn many interesting facts about the world, but it is more important to know who made the world and why. Since they are the most important things for us to know, God put these facts in the Bible. We know what the Bible says is true.

The first verse in the Bible says, "In the beginning God created the heaven and the earth." This does not tell us how long ago it happened. We do not need to know. But it is important to know God made the world, so He told us He did.

In this lesson we shall study other facts that God wants us to know about the world He created.

The earth, God's Word tells us, was without form. It was covered with darkness. And the Bible tells us that the Spirit of God moved upon the waters and God spoke. Now God, by simply speaking, can bring a thing into being. "Let there be light," He commanded. And what happened? There was light. The first day and the first night came into being.

The second day God spoke again. He caused the atmosphere to separate from the waters. More separation took place the next day, for at that time God caused the waters to gather together, and the dry land appeared. Then from the earth came forth grass and trees to cover the earth.

But as yet no sun, moon, nor stars were visible. But on the fourth day God commanded that there be lights in the sky—a greater light to shine by day, and a lesser light to shine by night. The greater light was the sun; the lesser was the moon. God placed stars in the heavens, too.

But how is it we have the birds in the sky and the living creatures in the sea? God created them. And how did God do it? He spoke, and what He commanded came into being.

"Let the waters bring forth abundantly the moving creature that hath life, and fowl that may fly above the earth in the open firmament of heaven," He said. So all kinds of living creatures were created to live in the rivers and seas. Many birds filled the air. This was the fifth day.

On the sixth day God made the animals. But the animals were not the whole of God's work that day. For on this sixth day God said, "Let us make man in our image, after our likeness: and let them have dominion over the fish of the sea, and over the fowl of the air, and over the cattle, and over all the earth, and over every creeping thing that creepeth upon the earth."

So God created man, making him in the image of God. That is, God gave man a nature that knows right from wrong. He gave him the ability to know, to love, and to serve God. He gave him a conscience. He even gave him the power of choice, which makes him responsible to God for all he does.

On the seventh day God rested. His acts of creation were finished. Every act of God's creation was great. But His greatest creation was not the earth, nor the things in the earth. His greatest creation was man.

This wonderful God of ours who brought the earth into being by simply speaking the word, still does mighty, wonderful things today. He can, by speaking the word, bring light and life to a heart full of darkness. Have you let Him bring eternal life into your heart?

THE BIRTH OF JESUS

The roads leading into Bethlehem were crowded. According to a law proclaimed by the emperor, everyone had to go to his native city to be enrolled; so, from all over the little land of Palestine, people were making their way back to the places where they had been born.

Among these travelers were Mary and Joseph. As the day was coming to its close, and night was rapidly settling down over the hillsides, they hurried along. They were tired—very tired. It was good now to be nearing Bethlehem. They were eager to find shelter for the night so they could rest.

But the city was filled with people. Joseph looked first in one place, then another. The inns (hotels) were full. At last, one innkeeper said they might sleep in his stable.

During that night a most wonderful thing happened. God sent His only begotten Son, the Lord Jesus Christ, into the world. The baby was named Jesus. An angel had told Joseph to do so. He was called "Jesus" because He had come to save His people from their sins.

Mary wrapped the Baby Jesus round and round with long pieces of cloth called swaddling clothes. That was the custom in those days. Then she laid Him in the manger.

That very night, out in the fields near Bethlehem, some shepherds were watching their sheep. Some slept while others watched. Then they changed places, and those who had been sleeping took their places, watching so no wild beasts could harm their sheep.

Suddenly a bright light shone round them. In the midst of the light they saw an angel. Frightened, they fell on their faces, scarcely daring to look up.

"Fear not," said the angel. "Behold, I bring you good tidings of great joy, which shall be to all people. For unto you is born this day in the city of David a Saviour which is Christ the Lord. And this shall be a sign unto you; Ye shall find the babe wrapped in swaddling clothes, lying in a manger."

Then suddenly the sky was filled with a multitude of angels who began praising God and saying, "Glory to God in the highest, and on earth peace, good will toward men."

Then, just as suddenly as the angels had come, they went back to heaven.

The shepherds talked about this wonderful news they had just heard.

"Let us now go even unto Bethlehem and see Him," they said. So they hurried to Bethlehem. There they found the Baby Jesus lying in a manger. He was wrapped in swaddling clothes, just as the angel had said He would be. There was no doubt about it. This Baby was God's own Son.

The shepherds went out and told everywhere how the angels had appeared and announced the birth of the Saviour. Gladly they told that they themselves had seen Him. They gave God praise and thanksgiving for all they had heard and seen. How wonderful it was that God had sent such a Gift to the world. They, too, could sing with the angels, "Glory to God in the highest!"

VICTORY OVER TEMPTATION

"If only I can make Jesus sin!" Satan said. He knew if Jesus sinned, then He could not be the Saviour. If Jesus sinned, His blood, though He died on the cross, would not take away sin. So again and again for forty days the devil tempted Jesus to sin in some way.

During those days of temptation, Jesus fasted. For forty days and forty nights, Jesus didn't even eat bread. By the time those forty days and nights had passed Jesus was very hungry.

Satan knew Jesus was hungry. "This is my chance to trick Him!" he thought.

"If you really are the Son of God, make some bread out of these stones. You know God can do anything," Satan said.

That was true. Jesus could have made bread out of the stones, for He is divine, and God can do anything. But Jesus knew He was not to use His power just to please Himself. He was to use it exactly as the Father in heaven directed Him. So now He controlled His appetite. He refused to work a miracle as Satan told Him to.

"It is written, Man shall not live by bread alone," Jesus said to Satan. Jesus knew God's Word and told Satan what the Scriptures said. Satan had no answer then.

In the first temptation Jesus had overcome Satan by quoting God's Word. So, in the second temptation, Satan used Scripture, cleverly leaving out part of the verse to make it seem to say something different from what God really had said. He said, "Don't you know you are God's Son? Go to Jerusalem. Climb to the very highest place in the temple—where all the people can see you. Then jump down. Show them how great you are! God will not let you get hurt. He will send angels to catch you."

But Jesus knew the Word of God, too. He knew that Satan had quoted only part of what the Scripture said. Jesus answered, "It is written again, thou shalt not tempt the Lord thy God."

Jesus had resisted the temptation to show off His power. Satan had to try something else. This time he took Jesus to a high mountain and showed Him all the kingdoms of the world.

"If you will fall down and worship me, I will give you all of these," Satan promised.

But Jesus resisted the temptation to get something by doing wrong. He was determined to do what God wanted Him to do. This meant going to the cross to die for the sins of the world. He did not yield to the temptation to avoid the cross and take the easy way.

"Go away!" commanded Jesus, "the Bible says that we must worship and serve only God."

Jesus had won the battle over Satan. He had overcome Satan's attempt to get Him in his control. God sent angels to comfort Jesus after this terrible temptation.

Since Jesus defeated Satan, He is able to help us when Satan tempts us. He understands about every temptation we have. We have only to call upon Him and He will help us gain the victory over Satan, no matter how Satan may tempt us.

We must defeat Satan in time of temptation. We please God when we resist Satan and do right instead of wrong. We become stronger in character, too, so we defeat the next temptation more easily. But to yield to temptation is sin.

The secret of winning in time of temptation is trusting Jesus and then depending on His help and strength.

Jimmie met a bully one day on his way home from school. This bully pushed Jimmie down in the mud.

Jimmie was trying not to cry when he felt someone touch his shoulder, lift him to his feet, and wipe the mud from his face with a clean handkerchief. This person took the bully by the collar and said, "If you ever touch my brother again, I'll take care of you!"

Jimmie was not afraid of the bully after that. He knew his big brother was bigger than the bully and that he would protect him. Jesus is our Big Brother who wants us to trust Him when we are tempted. He has already settled with Satan. So even though Satan may tempt us, he cannot make us do wrong.

JESUS TEACHES ABOUT SALVATION

Nicodemus, a ruler among the Jews, had a high position in the synagogue. He had heard of Jesus and believed that Jesus was going to have a kingdom. If so, he wanted to be in it. So one night he made his way down through the streets of Jerusalem to the house where Jesus was.

"Rabbi," he said, "we know that thou art a teacher come from God: for no man can do these miracles that thou doest, except God be with him."

Jesus heard the words Nicodemus spoke. But Jesus looked way down deep into Nicodemus' heart and saw that what he really wanted to know was how he could become a part of Jesus' kingdom.

"Verily, verily, I say unto thee, except a man be born again, he cannot see the kingdom of God," Jesus told him.

Nicodemus was puzzled. He did not understand what Jesus meant.

In school you have learned, perhaps, of different kinds of kingdoms. You can tell by what things are like whether they belong to the animal, vegetable, or mineral kingdom.

But Jesus spoke of another kingdom—the kingdom of God. To be a part of that kingdom people must receive from spiritual life or God-life. No person can make himself a member of the family or kingdom of God any more than a potato can make itself into a cat, or a diamond can change itself into a rose. We must receive this life from God.

Adam and Eve had this life when God created them. Then they sinned, and the spiritual part of them died. Since then, all people are born without this God-life. But any person can receive it from God. God has put within every person something that can know God when the Spirit of God makes it live. That part of us we call our spirit. Until our spirit is "made alive" by the Holy Spirit, we are "dead in trespasses and sins."

When we realize we are sinners, and that we need to have God put His life in us, we can come to Jesus and tell Him so. If we are truly sorry for our sins and are determined to live in obedience to Him, He forgives our sins and makes our spirits alive. We receive God's life into our spirit, and His life makes us alive spiritually. We call this being born again. This spiritual birth is the new birth. When we receive it we become a part of God's new kingdom.

"How can these things be?" asked Nicodemus. Perhaps you want to know also. How can you have this new birth? What must you do to have God put His life into you? Do you know?

To explain to Nicodemus how he could receive this new birth, Jesus reminded him of a story Nicodemus knew well. A long time ago, in the days when the children of Israel were being brought out of Egypt, they sinned very greatly. Because of this, God sent fiery serpents to bite the people, and many of them died.

Those who were left were very frightened. They asked Moses to pray for them.

"Make a serpent of brass and put it upon a pole," God told Moses. "Everyone who looks on the serpent of brass shall live." Moses did as God said. When the people looked upon the brass serpent on the pole, God healed them.

Jesus said to Nicodemus, "As Moses lifted up the serpent in the wilderness, even so must the Son of man be lifted up: That whosoever believeth on Him should not perish, but have eternal life. For God ... gave his only begotten Son, that whosoever believeth in him should not perish, but have everlasting life."

Jesus meant that He was going to have to be lifted up to die on the cross. Those who wished to receive eternal life, to be saved from sin, to have the new birth, were to believe on Jesus. When they did this, God would save them. He would give them spiritual life. They would be born again. The Israelites had only to look at the serpent to be healed. Sinners have only to believe on Jesus, and He will give them the kind of life that makes them children of God.

Had Jesus said to some very wicked person, "Ye must be born again," we might think that just some people need to be born again. But Nicodemus was a religious man. He knew the Scriptures. He always went to church. He was interested in spiritual things. Yet he was not ready for heaven. He had to receive Jesus into his heart and be born again if he wanted to become a child of God.

JESUS HEALS A BOY

In Capernaum there lived a nobleman. He was probably a member of the king's court. But for all his wealth and importance, his heart was very heavy. His boy was very, very sick.

Jesus had been healing people, and the news of His miracles had been carried far and wide. Jesus now was again in Cana, where He had turned the water into wine. The nobleman heard that Jesus was there.

"Jesus is in Cana. Oh, I do wish He would come here." Those could have been the nobleman's words.

"I will make the journey to Cana and ask Jesus to come here to Capernaum and make my boy well," the nobleman decided. He set out as fast as he could go to get to Jesus, for the boy was sick enough to die.

At last the worried father reached Cana. He hurried to Jesus. He was used to ordering other people about, but now he stood before Jesus very humbly.

"O Jesus, please come to Capernaum. My boy is very, very sick," he said. "He is about to die."

If the man expected Jesus to start off with him right away, he must have been disappointed. For Jesus answered, "Except ye see signs and wonders, ye will not believe."

The nobleman did not deny the fact he had come because of the signs and wonders he had heard about. But he was anxious to have Jesus come with him. If only they could get there before the boy died! He said, "Sir, come down ere my child die."

It had never occurred to this officer that Jesus might heal the child while He was still there in Cana. But Jesus simply said, "Go thy way, thy son liveth."

The nobleman did not say a word. He just believed what Jesus said. He turned and started home. Now he was believing, not because of the wonderful things he had heard about, but because of what Jesus had said.

The journey home was long. The nobleman was

believing what Jesus said. No doubt he kept thinking to himself, "My boy is going to live! Jesus said so. Whatever Jesus says is true. My boy is going to get well!"

As the man drew near his home, he saw some people coming toward him. They were his servants. These servants were coming to bring him some news.

"Your son liveth!" they told him.

"When did he begin to get better?" asked the nobleman.

"Yesterday, at the seventh hour," was the answer.

The father knew that was the very hour when Jesus had said, "Thy son liveth!"

The father was happy, of course. So was the rest of the family. The father knew only one who was divine could do what Jesus had done. He had believed Jesus could heal his son. Now he believed Jesus to be God's Son. He was ready to trust this Jesus, the Son of God, to follow Him, to serve Him. Today Jesus is still healing people who have faith.

JESUS STOPS A STORM

Jesus had taught and helped the people all day long. Evening came, and Jesus was very, very tired.

"Let us go over to the other side of the sea," Jesus said to His disciples. He went into the ship, and His disciples followed. Off they sailed. Jesus lay down in the bottom of the ship and went fast asleep.

By and by some clouds rose in the sky. Soon more arose. They became dark and threatening. Then the wind began to blow, changing the calm sea to one filled with ripples and waves. These small waves became large ones. Soon the whole sea was rolling with great waves that tossed the little ship about like a cork in a pan of swishing water. At first this alarmed the disciples. Then they became really frightened. And Jesus still slept.

"This storm is going to upset our ship, and we shall all be drowned," they thought.

Jesus always seemed to know just what to do in every situation. Now they wished He was awake. How could He sleep in such a storm, anyway! It would help just to know He realized their danger. They finally went to Jesus and awakened Him.

"Carest Thou not that we perish?" they asked.

How grieved Jesus must have been that they would think even for one moment that He would not care for them.

Jesus arose. Then He spoke to the sea!

"Peace, be still," He said.

The big tossing waves stopped rolling immediately. The wind stopped blowing. The sea became perfectly quiet. All was calm.

This astonished the disciples. They had seen Jesus heal the sick, so they knew He had power over disease. He had turned water into wine. But now He had shown His control over even the winds and the waves.

"What manner of man is this that even the winds and the sea obey Him!" they exclaimed.

Jésus is different from any other person. He is God in the form of man. He has all power. The wind, the sea, sickness, and even death must obey when Jesus speaks. But God has given each of us the power of choice. God wants us to obey Him, not because we must, but because we choose to do so. God only asks of us that which is for our good. When we obey, He wants it to be because we have chosen to do so. If any person chooses to disobey he is a greater loser. Only those who choose to obey have peace and true happiness.

Trouble comes sometimes even to those who do love Jesus. But Jesus can help us today just as He helped the disciples that day on the sea.

A group of boys had been camping on the lake for a week. The next day they would pack their things in the big truck and start for home.

Toward noon, dark clouds began to gather in the east. They covered the sky rapidly. Peals of thunder shook the air! Scattered streaks of lightning burst like Fourth of July rockets. A slow drizzle turned into a hard, driving rain. The wind swept in off the lake. Large breakers rolled and washed over the shore line.

The boys' tents snapped and popped as they strained at the ropes that held them.

"Looks like this one is going to be rough. Think we ought to try to make it home?" asked one of the fellows.

"Yes! We'll be swamped if we stay here. Look at those waves! They're getting worse, too."

They quickly pulled the stakes, rolled the beds, and stacked all the camp equipment in the truck.

Jim crawled into the driver's seat and called out, "Everybody hold on. We've got to make that cut before the tide gets too high."

But they could not make it. They turned and headed into the woods to get away from the shore line. The storm continued. About midnight it reached its height. By that time water covered the ground so they could no longer sit under the truck. Up it came until it almost reached the truck floor.

The boys looked at one another and realized the

danger they were in. Then one of the boys said, "Fellows, let's not be scared. We love God, and Jesus is with us. He can help us if we trust Him. He took care of His disciples during a storm on a sea one time. If He could stop the wind and waves on the Sea of Galilee, He can stop this water from rising."

The boys prayed. And God answered. The next morning the roar of a plane awakened the sleeping boys. It circled them a few times, then left. But in a few hours a Coast Guard cutter reached them.

The people of the little town gathered to welcome them home. The boys testified, "God answered prayer and stilled the wind and water for us last night, or we would not be here today."

JESUS TEACHES HOW TO PRAY

One day the disciples came to Jesus and said, "Lord, teach us to pray."

Now these disciples were Jews. They had prayed three times a day ever since they were very small. But they saw that Jesus was able to talk with God in a way that they couldn't. They wanted to learn how to have closer fellowship with God. They longed to know better how to pray, so God would answer their prayers.

So it was in answer to their own requests that Jesus gave them the model prayer. Often we call it "The Lord's Prayer." Using it as a pattern, we can learn better how to pray.

We are to come to God as we would to a good father here on earth. Good fathers love their children. They like to have their children talk with them. And God, the heavenly Father, is pleased when any person stops to talk with Him. For prayer is just that—talking to God as simply as if we were talking to our own earthly father.

Many people think of prayer as something they do to get something they want. But Jesus taught that all prayer should begin with worship of God. This should be a time of telling God of our love and appreciation. Not just for the blessings He sends, but who He is.

But we are to make requests, too. And we should begin by praying for the most important thing in all the world—that God's will be done here on earth as it is in heaven.

But aren't we to ask for the things we want? Yes, if we are sure that they are things God wants us to have. Jesus does not promise to answer just any prayer we pray. He promises to answer only those that are according to His will. We ourselves must be abiding in Him when we pray. That is, we must be living to please Him in all that we do. We must be sure that we have confessed and put away all wrongdoing, and that we are obeying His teachings.

Then, too, we must ask what we ask "in His name." That means we must be so one with Him that we are asking nothing that He is not willing to join us in asking the Father.

Making sure of all this, we are then ready to pray. And we must keep praying until the answer comes. For God is not only willing to answer our prayers. He is eager to do so! Satan can hinder a prayer from being answered for a time. We do not have to pray again and again to make God willing to answer our prayers. We do need to co-operate with God against Satan, and we do so by praying. Satan has to quit hindering if we keep praying. He does not have to, nor will he, if we grow discouraged and quit asking.

To help us understand the need for asking again and again, Jesus told of a man whose friend came to his house at midnight. He had no food, and it was the custom to eat bread with the man before going to bed.

He went to a neighbor's house and asked for three loaves of bread. But the neighbor was tired, and it was a great lot of trouble to get up and open the heavy door. So the neighbor said, "Don't bother me."

But the man kept a continuous rat-tat-tat on the door. Finally the neighbor could stand it no longer. He got up and got the bread for his friend.

Jesus said that though the neighbor would not get the man the bread because he was his friend, he did so because of the continual knocking. And if a person can get what he wants from someone unwilling to be bothered, how much more ought we to persist in praying to our loving heavenly Father, who is more willing to give than we are to ask.

We need never wonder if God will answer prayers that are according to His will. We need only to make sure that we keep asking until the answer comes.

JESUS THE KING

Jesus had never moved among the people as their king. The people knew Him only as their Friend, Teacher, and Healer.

When the time for the Passover feast drew near, Jesus said to the disciples, "Go into the village. There you will find a colt tied. Loose him, and bring him here. If any one asks why you are loosing him, just tell them that the Lord needs him."

The disciples found the colt just where Jesus had told them, and brought it to Him. Jesus rode this colt into Jerusalem. He had no royal coach, no rich robes. His only saddle was the garments His loving disciples had put on the donkey's back. Jesus wore no jewels or crown. Even the colt upon which He sat was borrowed.

In the East, the donkey is held in high esteem. It was more stately, livelier, and swifter than our donkey today. Every Jew expected his Messiah to come riding on one of these lowly creatures, for Zechariah the prophet had foretold that He would.

It was the custom for the people to greet a king by throwing flowers and foliage on his pathway. So, when Jesus came riding on a donkey, the crowd responded, hailing Him as their King. Some threw down their coats on the road. Others cut down branches and spread them in the way. The religious leaders at Jerusalem were unfriendly to Jesus, but there were people now in Jerusalem from all parts of Palestine. Many of them had seen Jesus heal in their villages, and they had listened to His teaching. They, perhaps, were the ones who went out of the city to meet Jesus.

"Hosanna!" they shouted. "Blessed be the King that cometh in the name of the Lord: peace in heaven, and glory in the highest."

But Jesus was not ready to reign from a throne of gold just then. He had come to be Saviour and Lord, forgiving sin, and reigning in the hearts of those who received Him.

Jesus is like a nobleman who went on a long journey. Before this nobleman left, he gave each of his servants an equal amount of money. They were to use that money to make more for their master.

The nobleman left and was gone quite some time. When he returned, he called his servants before him.

Each had to give account of how much he had made for his master. Then the nobleman rewarded each one according to the gain he had made.

Jesus has gone to heaven. Some day He will return. We have been left here to tell others of Him and to use our abilities so others will come to honor Him. When He returns, each Christian will be asked to show Jesus how he has spent his life. Those who have done much for Jesus will be rewarded accordingly. Jesus will richly reward every person who has yielded his life to Jesus, using his hands, feet, and mouth to serve the Lord rather than to live selfishly for himself.

WHY JESUS DIED

Just outside Pilate's judgment hall thronged a great mass of dark-faced, scowling Jews. They waited with determination for just one thing. They wanted Pilate to condemn Jesus to death.

"For what crime?" Pilate had asked.

It never would have done to tell Pilate the real reason why they wanted to put Jesus to death. So these Jews did not answer Pilate's question but falsely accused Jesus of many things. Their accusations contradicted one another, and Pilate knew Jesus was not guilty of any crime.

"I find in him no fault at all," Pilate told them.

That should have settled the matter. But it didn't. Pilate himself was guilty of certain crimes against the Jews. If he opposed them, they might rise up against the government. Then there would be trouble with Caesar. He wanted, in this case, to do the right thing, but he wanted still more to keep the favor of the people.

"It is customary to release a prisoner at the time of the Passover," Pilate told the people. "Whom will you that I release, Jesus or Barabbas?" Barabbas was a hardened criminal.

Pilate hoped the people would say, "Release Jesus." Surely they would not want so vile a man as Barabbas set free. But no, the people demanded that Barabbas be released.

Then Pilate made one last attempt to make the Jews willing to release Jesus. He ordered Jesus scourged. When the scourging was over, Pilate had Jesus brought out to the people. He hoped that when they saw blood flowing from His back where the cruel lashes had cut deeply into His body and when they saw the blood flowing down His face from the thorny crown that had been pushed down on His head, they would change their minds.

But no. These people had no pity, they were so wicked. Their hearts were filled with jealousy and anger because Jesus had dared to preach against their sins.

"Crucify Him! Crucify Him! If you let this man go, you aren't Caesar's friend," they shouted. "Whosoever maketh himself a king speaketh against Caesar."

So, rather than displease the Jews and risk the danger of an uprising, Pilate ordered Jesus crucified.

Out to Golgotha the Roman soldiers took our Lord. There, between two thieves, they nailed Him to the cross. About three o'clock in the afternoon, Jesus gave up His life.

God had allowed His Son to be crucified. Do you know why? Because sin had separated man from God. Jesus took upon Himself on the cross all the sins of the world. He gave up His life that He might bring us to God. He died for everything about us that is ungodly—our selfishness, our bad tempers, our jealousy, our lying. Because He took upon Himself every person's sins, anyone who will can now draw near God. Jesus, in dying for us on the cross, has made it possible for us to live again in harmony and fellowship with God.

JESUS, THE RISEN LORD

After Jesus died on the cross, Joseph of Arimathaea took Jesus' body and laid it in his own tomb. Then he rolled a great stone across the door, and left.

Jesus had said He would be raised from the dead. But Jesus' friends had forgotten this. His enemies remembered though, and they were afraid He would do just this. So they went to Pilate. They pretended they were afraid that Jesus' disciples would steal His body out of the tomb and say He had risen.

"Place soldiers to watch the tomb," they said.

"Very well," Pilate told them, "make it as secure as you can."

So Roman soldiers went to guard the tomb. But early on Sunday morning, the earth began to quake. An angel of the Lord came and rolled away the stone that sealed the tomb. In the presence of the angel, the guards shook and became like dead men. And Jesus rose from the dead, a conqueror of death and the grave.

Early on that Sunday morning two women, Mary and Mary Magdalene, came to the tomb. As they came near the tomb, they noticed first of all that the stone which closed the tomb was rolled aside. On it sat the angel whose appearance was like lightning and whose garments were white as snow.

"Fear not," said the angel. "I know that ye seek Jesus, which was crucified. He is not here: for he is risen, as he said. Come, see the place where the Lord lay. And go quickly, and tell the disciples that he is risen from the dead." Then the angel added. "He goeth before you into Galilee; there shall ye see him." The women left the tomb quickly to go and tell the disciples the glorious news.

Jesus was alive! The women hurried away, eager to tell the glorious news they had just received. Then a most wonderful thing happened. Jesus Himself met them.

"All hail," said Jesus.

The women held Him by the feet and worshiped.

"Don't be afraid," said Jesus. "Go tell my brethren to go into Galilee, and there they shall see me."

Meanwhile the guards went to the priests and told them what had happened. The priests were very upset when they learned of the earthquake and of the now empty tomb.

Rather than let the people know of Jesus' resurrection and have them believe He is God's Son, the priests decided to pay the Roman soldiers to lie about the matter.

"Say that His disciples came and stole away His body while you slept," the Jewish leaders ordered.

The soldiers took the money and told what they had been paid to say. But their lies did not change the truth. Jesus had arisen from the dead. He is alive, even today.

Because Jesus lives, we may have Him with us at all times. Because He was resurrected we know that even though we may die, we, too, will be resurrected.

THE COMING OF THE HOLY SPIRIT

Several days after His resurrection Jesus went back to heaven. Just before He left, He said to the disciples, "Go back to Jerusalem and wait for the promise of the Father. Ye shall be baptized with the Holy Ghost before many days.... Ye shall receive power after the Holy Ghost is come upon you. Then you will be witnesses unto me both in Jerusalem ... and unto the uttermost part of the earth."

The disciples were obedient. They went to an upper room in Jerusalem. There they waited for the Holy Spirit Jesus had promised to send.

Up to this time, the Holy Spirit had come only upon Jews, and upon only a few of them whom God had chosen. Now God was ready to call out, from every nation, all people who would love and serve Him. He was ready to send the Holy Spirit upon all these people, regardless of their race or nationality, thus forming on earth the Church.

Ten days after the ascension, which was fifty days after the Passover (the day on which Jesus was crucified), the Holy Spirit was poured out. Suddenly there was a sound that filled all the house in which those who had been waiting for the Holy Spirit were sitting. It was like a rushing mighty wind. Tongues like fire sat upon each of them. Then the most glorious thing happened. All these people began to speak in strange languages. Each one of them began speaking words he had never spoken before.

At this time there were Jews in Jerusalem from "every nation under heaven." They came running to see what was happening. How surprised they were to hear these Christians speaking their languages.

"Are not all these which speak Galileans?" they

asked. How then could they speak their languages? Awe filled their hearts as they heard the people praising God in other languages.

While amazement filled the hearts of many who listened, there were some who became scornful at what they were hearing.

"These men are full of new wine," they scoffed.

Then Peter began to prophesy. He stepped out before the crowd and began to speak to them in his own language. He reminded them that Joel had prophesied this very thing years before. In fact, it had been 800 years since Joel had foretold the outpouring of the Spirit. In that prophecy God had said, "I will pour out my spirit upon all flesh. Your sons and your daughters shall prophesy, and your young men shall see visions, and your old men shall dream dreams:

"And on my servants and on my handmaidens I will pour out in those days of my Spirit; and they shall prophesy."

"This is that which was spoken by the prophet Joel," Peter told them.

Then Peter went on to tell them that this outpouring of the Spirit was for all men, not just Jews. "The promise," Peter said, "is to all that are afar off, even to as many as the Lord shall call!"

That promise includes you. Today God is still pouring out His Spirit just as He did on the Day of Pentecost. People receive the baptism of the Holy Spirit, and when they do, they speak in other tongues just as they did on the Day of Pentecost.

Perhaps you are wondering what effect this wonderful experience will have upon your life. Here are a few things the Holy Spirit will do for us:

1. He will give us boldness to witness for Christ.

Peter was afraid to stand up for Jesus at His trial. But after he had received the Holy Spirit he was not afraid to stand up before thousands of people and tell them about his Lord. We, too, will receive boldness to tell others about Jesus when we have been filled with the Holy Spirit.

2. He will help us understand the Bible. The Holy Spirit helped Peter understand what Joel meant when he said God would pour out His Spirit upon all flesh. He also helped Peter to understand and explain many things in the Bible about Jesus. We will understand God's Word as never before when we have been baptized in the Holy Spirit.

3. He will make Jesus real to us. The Lord became so precious to Peter after his Pentecostal experience that he at once began preaching about Jesus. The Holy Spirit will make Jesus as real to us as He was to Peter!

4. He will help us win others for Christ. After Peter's mighty sermon on the Day of Pentecost, many were so stirred that they cried out, "What shall we do?" Of course, Peter and the other Christians were glad to tell them how to get saved. And that very day 3,000 people gave their hearts to Jesus! The Holy Spirit will help us make Christ so real to sinners that they will want to get saved.

5. He will bring joy and comfort to our hearts. Peter was not afraid to go to jail after he had been filled with the Spirit. One day he was beaten cruelly for preaching about Jesus. But he was so happy that he went away rejoicing!

Aren't you glad this wonderful gift is for us today? Let us start waiting upon God right now, and He will fill each heart just as He has promised.

PIONEERING IN
YOUR CHURCH

Many years ago a traveler happened through a village in Doubs, France. It was twilight time, and he noticed everybody rushing through the streets carrying bronze lamps. Curious about this, he stopped a villager and asked why everyone was carrying lamps and where they were going. In reply the villager said, "We are going to church, and we have no other way to light our building except the lamps we bring. When the church was erected in 1550, the town mayor decided that everyone should bring his own light. So now everyone goes to church to make it brighter. If anyone stays home, he knows the church will be darker and the service sadder."

Jesus said, "Ye are the light of the world." Although Jesus did not mean that we looked like lightbulbs, he did mean that our Christian life was like a bright light shining in a dark place. This is why it is so important for the Pioneer to attend church every time the door is open. If he misses, the church is a little darker, and the church service is sadder because one "light" is missing. When all the "lights" are there, the church will glow brightly with the full strength God intended for it. Then the ones who are in darkness will be able to see God through the light of the church.

A LIVE COAL

There is also another reason why it is important that each Pioneer should attend church regularly. This reason is that it is spiritually healthy to attend God's house. One time a church member failed to attend Sunday school. The Sunday school superintendent felt bad about the man missing and went to visit him. When the superintendent arrived at the man's home, he found him sitting in front of his fireplace watching the glowing coals.

Somewhat startled by the superintendent's visit, the absentee hastily placed a chair beside his and invited his visitor to be seated. Together the men sat down, and the one who had been absent waited nervously for the superintendent to scold him. However, the superintendent did not say a word. Rather he reached for the fireplace tongs, lifted a live coal from the midst of the fire and placed it on the hearthstone away from the flames. In a few minutes the coal that had been burning brightly died out. The absentee broke the silence and said, "You don't have to say a word. I see what you mean, and I will be there next Sunday."

Just as a coal taken from the fire dies out in a few moments, so will a Christian taken from the warm place of the church. A Christian, like the coal, may be on fire for God; but if he is taken away from those who love God as he does, he will soon die spiritually. This is why it is so important for Pioneers to attend church every time it is possible. Attending church will help you stay alive for God and will help you be a better Pioneer for Christ.

A PLACE TO MEET GOD

A few years ago when Franklin Roosevelt was President of these United States, his pastor received a telephone call from an anxious person. The man calling said, "Tell me, pastor, will the President be in church Sunday?" To this the pastor replied, "I don't know whether the President will be in church Sunday, but I do know that God will be there." Pioneers should attend each church service because God is there.

Only as you meet God can you grow in Him. And, where is a better place to meet God than church? As the Pioneer attends church, he is drawn to God and learns how to let God speak to his heart and direct his steps. In every service a Pioneer can meet God in a new and important way. So if you want to know God better, as every Pioneer does, you will want to attend church and be active in the church activities. This means you will want to attend all services for you such as children's church, vacation Bible school, clubs, and special meetings. You will also want to give to the church so the message of God can be taught to all men. This is a real sign of an outstanding Pioneer.

One of the greatest Pioneers of all times had some very important words to say about attending church. This man, who traveled all over the then-known world telling others about Christ, also practiced what he preached. The apostle Paul said, "Not forsaking the assembling of ourselves together, as the manner of some is; but exhorting one another: and so much the more, as you see the day approaching" (Hebrews 10:25).

PIONEERING IN
CHRISTIAN SERVICE

A tall young man piloted his crude boat down the swirling Ohio River. He was on a mission that he felt he was "called" to do, and he had with him one of the strangest cargoes ever shipped on that river. His small boat was filled with apple seeds, and his mission was to plant them in the early western frontier.

This man became a legend in his own time. Although his real name was John Chapman, he was better known to the pioneers as "Johnny Appleseed." Johnny spent his entire life and all his money traveling through the rugged pioneer country planting apple seeds.

Johnny Appleseed had grown to love delicious, red apples and felt he wanted everyone to share this God-given blessing. Starting out with his boat load of apple seeds, Johnny Appleseed planted thousands of trees throughout Pennsylvania, Ohio, and Indiana.

At night, when it was too dark to plant trees, Johnny would enter the homes of pioneers and share some of his experiences with them. Pioneers welcomed his visits because he would bring news of what was going on outside their little world. He would keep them informed about their neighbors whom they were able to see only once or twice a year. He would tell interesting stories to the youngsters about Indians, pioneer life, and about far-away and strange places. Often he would sit up with the family until the early hours of the morning telling them about many exciting things. Then before going to bed, Johnny Appleseed would get out his old worn Bible and read the Word of God to the pioneer families. He would explain to them the meaning of various Scriptures and tell them about the Christ that he had learned to love. Many of the pioneers could not read, so they were thrilled when Johnny would come and read to them about God.

One day in 1812, Johnny Appleseed arrived in Mansfield, Ohio. He had been planting trees all along his way and was tired. However, when he arrived in that area, he learned that Indians were going to attack that town. When night fell, Johnny dashed into the woods and started making his way toward Mount Vernon where soldiers were camped. It was 36 miles away through dark and dangerous forests. However, Johnny knew that he must risk his life if the town of Mansfield was to be saved from the Indians. Creeping and sometimes running through the woods, Johnny Appleseed hurried toward his destination. The woods were filled with Indians, and one slip might mean his life. The hours passed as he pushed his exhausted body on toward Mount Vernon. The sounds around him made him shudder. Once or twice he thought he heard Indians following him. Nevertheless, he continued on through the night. Finally he arrived at Mount Vernon, **aroused the army, and headed back with them to Mansfield. The army arrived just in time to defend the city from a terrible Indian massacre.**

Johnny Appleseed lived to be an old man, finally dying in Fort Wayne, Indiana. Many hundreds of pioneers mourned his passing because he had spent his entire life in their service. During his life he had planted thousands of apple trees that would be enjoyed for many years, brought cheer to many a lonely pioneer family, and introduced many to Christ. His was truly a life of Christian service.

This outstanding example of Christian service should inspire each Pioneer today to dedicate himself to the service of God by helping others. There are many things a Pioneer could do that would bring cheer to the lonely lives of people. Just as the pioneer spirit of helping others existed many years ago, it should exist today. In early pioneer days neighbors would gather to help friends build their barns or houses. When there were sick people, the pioneers would take food and medicine to them, often at the risk of their own lives. This is the true Pioneer and Christian spirit, a spirit you as a Pioneer can have. Talk with your Commander about how you can be of service to others.

PIONEERING IN
YOUR HOME

Have you thought how important your home is? It gives you food and a place to live in. It is the place where you first learn how to live with other people. And probably it was the first place where you were taught about God and Jesus. Read how David's home life helped him to meet and defeat the enemy.

HITTING THE MARK

"Stop, boy! Do you think I am a dog that can be chased with stones? By tonight the birds will be picking your flesh, and the animals will be eating you for supper."

Armed with five stones and a slingshot, these were the words David heard as he left the camp of God's army to battle with the heathen giant from the enemy's camp. But David had another weapon—God's guidance—that was not seen by the giant. This gave David great courage, and he replied, "Everyone here shall know that the Lord does not save with sword and spear: for the battle is the Lord's, and he will give you into our hands." (Read 1 Samuel 17.)

David knew his weapon would work, for he had tested it several times. While taking care of his father's sheep, he had been attacked by a bear and a lion. With God's help he had killed both of them. He knew that when you "acknowledge God in all your ways, he will direct your paths."

Without fear, David took a stone from his bag, put it in his slingshot, ran toward the giant, and threw the stone. With God's help the stone stayed on course and found its mark deep in the head of the giant, who fell on his face. Then with the giant's sword David cut off his opponent's head. All of the enemy fled, because they knew God was with David.

You, too, can hit the mark if you will be on God's side and let Him guide you. To do this you must start with your home life as David did.

Something to Do: Make a large target with six sections and label them (1) Prayer; (2) Bible reading; (3) Obey parents; (4) Clean body; (5) Good deeds; (6) Trust in God. Write the following Scripture references in the section to correspond with the numbers given:

(1) Matthew 21:22
(2) Psalm 119:11
(3) Ephesians 6:1
(4) Psalm 24:3-4
(5) Luke 6:31
(6) Proverbs 3:5

Make a dart out of a matchstick, a pin, tape, and paper fins. Leave the fins out and throw the dart, trying to stick it in the target. Then put the fins in and try again. See how important it is to have the right guidance. It is important that you look to God for His guidance.

Each day until you have hit all the sections in your target with your dart, learn the Scripture references given on your target. Then, each day for a week have your dad or mother check below for a good deed that you have done during the day and for obeying them during the day.

	Good Deed	Obeyed Parents
Monday		
Tuesday		
Wednesday		
Thursday		
Friday		
Saturday		
Sunday		

PIONEERING IN LIFE

You are important. You are important to your parents, to your friends, and most of all, you are important to God. We know you are important to God because he was willing for his Son to die for you. He paid the price for your life through Jesus. Now read how Big Jim paid the price for a friend.

Big Jim, as his friends called him, was sailing homeward. For three years he had lived a lonely life in the Klondike area of Alaska. His camp was located about 100 miles north of Dawson City. Jim was a prospector. He had gone to the Klondike with a fever for gold. After three years of washing sand out of the Klondike River, he had saved enough gold to weigh out $20,000. The gold was in a money belt tied around his waist.

As Jim looked over the railing of the ship and watched the boat plow through the water, his every thought was of home. As yet he had not decided just what he would do with all the money he would get when the gold dust was exchanged for dollars. Jim patted the heavy money belt about his waist. "Yep," he said aloud to himself, "it's all here."

Jim was running a risk carrying all this dust in the big money belt. But the risk would be worth the extra dollars he would get for selling in Seattle, Washington, rather than Fairbanks, Alaska. Then, too, Jim was not afraid of being robbed. He was big and strong; few men would ever dare to tackle Big Jim.

The trip had been very pleasant. In fact, Jim had enjoyed being with people. For three years he had lived alone, and the sight of people made him very happy. On the trip Jim made friends with a little six-year-old girl. She had long curls and big blue eyes. The two of them had become real friends.

Suddenly Jim was awakened from his thoughts by a loud scream. He felt the motors of the ship slacken their speed. Somebody yelled, "Man overboard." Jim looked over the rail, and there in the water he saw a little head bobbing on the surface. It was his little six-year-old friend. Without hesitating, Jim sprang like a cat into the water.

He splashed in the water near the girl. Only a few yards separated them. Big Jim tried to swim, but something held him back. It was the gold. He couldn't swim with all that gold dust tied around his waist. The weight held him back.

A decision had to be made. Jim must decide between the gold and the girl. Jim decided. He unbuckled the money belt, pulled it from around his waist and let it go. His big hands then lunged for the girl.

He had reached her in time. By now the lifeboat was being lowered from the steamer. Jim and his little friend stayed afloat until the boat reached them and they were pulled from the water.

When Jim handed the little girl to the crewmen in the lifeboat, he yelled out, "I lost the gold, but I saved a life."

Jim's little friend was important to him, and he was willing to pay a valuable price to save her life.

GROWING UP FOUR WAYS

Growing up! What a job that is. It is the most important thing any boy can do. It is not easy. But it is important because growing up means becoming a man. Have you ever thought about what kind of man you will become? You can tell, because the kind of man that you will become will depend on how you grow and develop day by day.

The Bible tells us that Jesus grew up four different ways. He grew in mind, in body, in His relationship to God, and in His relationship to people. (Learn Luke 2:52.) Ask your dad or mother to use the diagram below to explain how Jesus was a healthy and well-balanced person. Would this have been true if He had failed to grow in any of the four parts represented by the circle? (Check your answer.)

Yes .... No ....

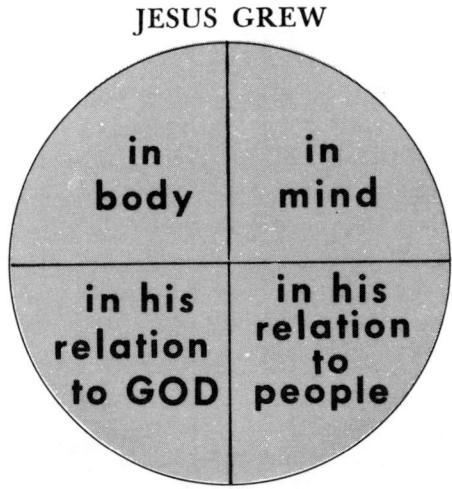

Something to Do: After talking with your parents, list as many things as you can that will help you grow and develop four ways.

These Will Help Me Grow Mentally	*These Will Help Me Grow Physically*
These Will Help Me Grow Socially	*These Will Help Me Grow Spiritually*

(Signed)

GOD'S PLAN FOR YOUR LIFE

Have you ever stopped to think that every great man at one time was a boy? Men like George Washington, Abraham Lincoln, David Livingstone, William Carey, and others were boys just like you and your friends. Probably they didn't realize they were to become great men, but God had a plan for their lives. Here is a true story of a boy who became a great world leader.

School was out and Dwight rushed down the street. His foot slipped and he fell, skinning his knee. Quickly Dwight got up, looked around, brushed himself off, and raced for home. The spill on the street was soon forgotten.

Two mornings later Dwight awoke with a terrible ache in his left leg. That evening his foot turned black. It was painful to take off his shoe and stocking. Dwight's mother and father looked at the boy and immediately sent for Dr. Conklin. The doctor examined the leg and traced with his finger a red streak from the knee to the foot.

"Blood poisoning," the doctor said. "It's serious."

When Dr. Conklin left the room, Dwight could hear voices down the hall. The doctor was saying something about tomorrow and something about maybe taking the leg off.

Dwight spent a sleepless night. Two things bothered him—the pain he was suffering and the thought of losing his leg.

Dr. Conklin returned the next morning and looked at the injured leg. He shook his head. Dwight looked at the doctor and clinched his teeth. The boy understood what the doctor was thinking about.

"If we do it now, we can save the leg above the

knee," the doctor said quietly. "The longer we wait the more we will have to take off."

Dwight shook his head strongly. "You won't take any off," he said.

"But it is the only possible way to save your life," the doctor tried to explain. "It won't be as bad as it sounds."

"No," Dwight said in a courageous voice. "I would rather die first."

Everyone left the room except Edgar, Dwight's brother. Dwight took Edgar's hand and pulled it desperately.

"You've got to promise me you won't let 'em do it," he sobbed. "You've got to promise. I won't be a cripple. I'd rather die." Solemnly Edgar promised not to let them take off his leg.

For two days and nights Edgar watched over his brother. At times Dwight did not know him, and he would scream out in pain. The doctor came again and again to look at the boy. The leg continued to swell. "Nothing we can do will save his life," said the doctor.

Prayer was not overlooked in this great hour of crisis. Dwight's mother and father prayed to God. They prayed that God would help their boy. Only a miracle could save his life.

The miracle came! The fever in the body of the sick boy began to leave. So did the swelling from the leg. Dwight awoke from a long sleep. He was alive and feeling better. Slowly he grinned at his brother and the others in the room. Three weeks later he was able to walk out of his room.

Dwight became a famous man—Dwight Eisenhower, the 34th President of the United States. God had great plans for his life. His life was to be used in many ways as he served not only his country, but the world.

You may or may not become President of the United States, as did Dwight Eisenhower. But remember, God has a plan for you and your life. Begin now to learn what that plan is and to prepare yourself to do what God wants you to do.

Scripture to Learn: Read 1 Samuel 3:1-10. Learn verse 10 by memory. Ask your dad or mother to discuss the meaning of this passage of Scripture with you.

FINDING YOUR REAL SELF

I guess everyone knows the stories of Rudolph, the Red Nosed Reindeer, and of the Ugly Duckling. Both of them were downhearted, thinking they were not much good, when actually their time had not arrived.

Some of our greatest athletes were weaklings as boys. Some of our greatest inventors were considered stupid by their teachers, and some of our greatest political leaders were failures in their early lives. I recall a story about an eagle that had been taken from its nest by a farmer when it was young. He clipped one wing so it could not fly away, and put it with the young chickens. It soon felt right at home with the chickens, ate chicken feed, and seemed almost like a chicken.

One day a visitor stopped at the farm and chanced to see the young eagle with the chickens. "Hey, where did you get that eagle," he asked. "What's it doing with the chickens?" "Well," the farmer replied, "maybe he was an eagle once, but he's a chicken now. He's been living with them so long, he even looks like a chicken. Even though his wing is grown, he'll never fly again."

"That's where you are wrong, my friend," said the visitor. "Once an eagle, always an eagle. I can get him to fly."

The farmer agreed to let him try, so the visitor caught the eagle. He held the eagle in his hands and talked to it. "You are an eagle. You belong to the sky." Tossing it as high in the air as he could, he shouted, "Now, fly." But the eagle floated down to earth and ate food again with the chickens.

This was a challenge to the visitor, so next morning he put the eagle in a sack and carried it up a mountain, determined to toss the eagle from the highest point of the cliff, if necessary, to make him fly. When taken from the sack, the eagle felt the wind of the mountain heights, caught the brightness of the sun, and saw itself high above the valley. It struggled free from the visitor's hands, spread its wings and went off the cliff. Now the eagle knew it was an eagle, and although it lost height at first, it started to circle and gradually rose higher and higher into the sky. It never returned to the farmer's yard to live with the chickens again.

Fellows, I am convinced that God has a plan for each of our lives. Some people discover the plan sooner than others, but when we do discover what that plan is, then we take off into the blue and become a part of God's great plan. We find our part in this great plan by doing our best every day, and by keeping our eyes and hearts alert, so that we can know His will for us.